YOU'RE NEVER ALONE

Marie Shropshire

HARVEST HOUSE PUBLISHERS
Eugene, Oregon 97402

YOU'RE NEVER ALONE

Copyright ©1996 by Marie Shropshire
Published by Harvest House Publishers
Eugene, Oregon 97402

Library of Congress Cataloging-in-Publication Data

Shropshire, Marie, 1921–
　　You're never alone / Marie Shropshire.
　　　　　p.　cm.
　　　　ISBN 1-56507-426-2 (alk. paper)
　　　　1. Presence of God—Meditations.　2. Consolation.　I. Title
BT180.P6S48　1996　　　　　　　　　　　　　　　　　　　95-44475
242—dc20　　　　　　　　　　　　　　　　　　　　　　　　CIP

98 99 00 01 02 03 — 10 9 8 7 6 5 4 3

This book is affectionately dedicated to
Susan
Jason
Amy
Whatever your future holds,
may you never feel lonely or separated
from the One who knows you best
and loves you most.

Contents

Preface

We all have times of loneliness. We all know how loneliness feels. But God never intends for us to be lonely. When trials come and God seems far away, He is really with us—beside us and inside us by His Spirit. He is always our faithful Friend.

Referring to Jesus, wise old Solomon said, "There is a friend who sticks closer than a brother" (Proverbs 18:24). Jesus encouraged His disciples (and us) with these words: "You are my friends if you do what I command.... I have called you friends" (John 15:14,15).

Our Friend Jesus gives us peace when we're troubled or fearful. We can share with Him our deepest secrets and be assured of His understanding. He is the Source of our joy and hope. If we accept His friendship, Jesus is a Friend who never leaves us alone.

1

*When Tragedy
Hits*

Peace I leave with you; my peace I give you. ... Do not let your hearts be troubled and do not be afraid (John 14:27).

Sudden death claimed the infant daughter of Nan and Wes. *Devastation* only mildly described their feelings. No one could answer their pain-filled questions. God alone could offer hope and comfort.

When the sorrows of life gnaw at your heart and you find no answers, know that there is hope. God is there, saturating your spirit with His peace. His mercies can cause you to feel His wonderful love gently healing you. In the midst of your sorrow, a new sense of identity can be yours as you realize how special you are to the heart of the heavenly Father.

Let your awareness of God's love be sufficient for your wounds until He heals your hurts completely. You feel your pain engulfing you, but His eternal love is greater. He says to you even now, "So do not fear, for I am with you; do not be dismayed, for I am your God. I will strengthen you and help you; I will uphold you with my righteous right hand" (Isaiah 41:10). You can be sure you are never alone, especially when you're hurting.

Whether you turn to the right or to the left, your ears will hear a voice behind you, saying, "This is the way; walk in it" (Isaiah 30:21).

When baseball pitcher Dave Dravecky lost his throwing arm to cancer, he told friends he was able to cope with his anguish only because of God's gift of grace and strength. He said, "I don't deserve it. I don't bring it about. It's a gift. And that is how I am able to cope."

When you doubt whether you can cope with your agony, be still and feel the touch of the Lord's hand guiding you, comforting you in your despair. Know that His gift of grace is present to strengthen you. He, too, felt pain. He can whisper to your heart and bring consolation.

He wants to help you find peace and joy in the midst of your heartache. He walks beside you at all times to speak comfort to your heart and to sustain you. His love cannot fail you.

"He rises to show you compassion" (Isaiah 30:18). In your weakness, He will show Himself strong in your behalf. He is never indifferent to your cry. He says to you now: "I, even I, am he who comforts you" (Isaiah 51:12).

No one whose hope is in [Him] will ever be put to shame (Psalm 25:3).

*C*harlotte Elliott turned away from the sunlight shining through her window. Physical pain had plunged her into emotional darkness. One day a visitor pointed her to the way of salvation. "Come just as you are," he explained. Charlotte accepted the invitation and her life was changed. Her emotional darkness soon came to an end. Inspired by the words of her friend, many years later she wrote the well-known hymn "Just As I Am."

You can find comfort in remembering that the One who invites you to come just as you are feels what you feel. He suffers every heartache with you. He is your never-failing help. Fix your hope in Him during your hours of darkness. His mercies can shine through the windows of your heart.

Since the One who made heaven and earth is over all, you can be assured He is in charge of your life—if you will let Him be. He will not fail you or let you down. You can cling to Him in confidence, regardless of how dark and hopeless your situation looks.

The Spirit of the Lord is upon Me, because He has anointed Me to preach the gospel to the poor. He has sent me to heal the broken-hearted . . . to set at liberty those who are oppressed (Luke 4:18 NKJV).

*W*hen Jesus spoke these words, He was declaring that He came to fulfill the prophecy of Isaiah 61. Jesus never doubted that God had sent Him to heal the brokenhearted and those who were oppressed for any reason. These words of Jesus are as much for you as for the people to whom He spoke them.

Jesus came to free all who are captive to the power of pain and brokenness. That was and is His purpose. Your relationship with God entitles you to all His magnificent resources. When your circumstances have you feeling the most oppressed and the most brokenhearted, remind yourself of the purpose of the coming of Jesus: to heal the broken-hearted.

You often feel tossed to and fro. Jesus knows. He knows and cares. You can come to Him with your broken heart and find rest and comfort. He has a place for your broken heart in His heart of love.

The LORD longs to be gracious to you; he rises to show you compassion. For the LORD is a God of justice. Blessed are all who wait for him! (Isaiah 30:18).

*J*oseph Girzone tells of going to a nursing home with his mother to visit her friend Anna whom she had not seen in many years. When his mother saw Anna confined to a bed and twisted with pain, she started to cry. The paralyzed woman said, "If you're crying for me, don't. God is so close to me all the time. I don't think I could be happier."

Suffering, whether physical or emotional, seems to bring us to a relationship with the Lord which we could never attain in any other way. God is not the author of suffering, but He is able to use it for our good.

Your situation may tempt you to believe that God has forgotten you. He hasn't. He will make a way for you. He works in ways you cannot see. He "is able to do immeasurably more than all we ask or imagine" (Ephesians 3:20). God wants all of His children to live a life of joy. He offers us hope, peace, joy, and love.

... your faith—of greater worth than gold, which perishes even though refined by fire—may be proved genuine and may result in praise, glory and honor when Jesus Christ is revealed (1 Peter 1:7).

*T*he whole world was shaken by the news of the horrible bombing which occurred in Oklahoma City in 1995. Most of us ached with sorrow for those who suffered the loss of loved ones and property. Many asked, "Where was God? Why did He allow such a tragedy to happen?"

We know God never causes tragedies. He allows them to happen because He gives to all men—the evil as well as the righteous—a free will. But His heart is touched with the grief of those who suffer.

Regardless of what may come, we are not to allow anything to shake our faith in God. Our faith is of "greater worth than gold," and it sometimes must be "refined by fire." We are never alone. In the midst of all of life's tragedies and tribulations, God wants us to know He is present to comfort and encourage us. "For the LORD comforts his people and will have compassion on his afflicted ones" (Isaiah 49:13).

2

When God Seems Far Away

I have told you these things, so that in me you may have peace. In this world you will have trouble. But take heart! I have overcome the world (John 16:33).

"Last year was the worst year of my life," a friend wrote. Another said, "I never could have made it through the past year if I had not known the Lord was with me every moment."

Struggles seem to be the stuff of life for most of us. Jesus knew we would experience problems. That's why He told us to expect trouble and to take heart. Knowing that Jesus promises peace when the world offers little but difficulty enables us to handle life's blows when they come.

I must remind myself that Jesus conquered the world and deprived it of its power to harm. Since He won the war, I can win my battles. If I focus on circumstances, I sink in frustration. That's why I try to remember these lines:

> Never a trial that He is not there,
> Never a burden that He doth not bear,
> Never a sorrow that He doth not share,
> Moment by moment, I'm under His care.

He is your shield and helper and your glorious sword (Deuteronomy 33:29).

A little girl had moved with her family to a new home near a forest. Late one afternoon she went for a walk and got lost. To find her way home proved impossible. When darkness approached, she feared she would have to spend the night alone. But her parents came to her rescue.

When you feel hopelessly lost, God will come to your rescue. He will intervene in your impossible situations. Although invisible, God is no less real. He will release you from your bondage of fear, anxiety, and loneliness.

God invites you to bring your feelings of lostness to Him. He is ever-present to remind you of His unconditional love and faithfulness. You can talk to God anywhere and anytime. You can look into His Word and find promises to fit your needs of the moment.

Quieting yourself in His presence will help to remind you that He is your Shield and Helper. When you need Him most, you may *feel* that He is far away. But that's when He most wants you to know that He is your ever-present Helper. Wherever you go and whatever you feel, the Lord is with you.

Because of the LORD's great love we are not consumed, for his compassions never fail. They are new every morning; great is your faithfulness (Lamentations 3:22,23).

*J*eremiah felt great anguish of soul because of the circumstances in his life and surroundings. He felt alone and helpless. In his discouragement he turned to God. He didn't attempt to hide his feelings of anger and despair from God. At one point he said in effect, "All hope is gone for the Lord has left me. I can never forget these awful years."

After expressing his feelings, Jeremiah reflected upon God's faithfulness. He knew in reality that God had not left him. He realized that God's love is unfailing.

Your inner pain may cause you to feel as if God has left you and that you are about to be consumed. But you have the promise of the Lord's great love. He will not allow you to be consumed. You may be tempted to doubt that God cares, but His compassionate heart remains the same—unchanging in faithfulness to you.

God still restores His people. As He heard Jeremiah's prayer and eventually restored Israel, He will restore you.

Can a mother forget the baby at her breast and have no compassion on the child she has borne? Though she may forget, I will not forget you! (Isaiah 49:15).

*I*stood at my living-room window, watching two little figures until they disappeared down the street. They looked so small and defenseless against the big world. One was a six-year-old boy, the other a girl almost eight. Each carried a book satchel in one hand and a lunch box in the other.

Many years have passed since that disquieting day when I was required to trust my priceless human treasures for the better part of the day to someone else's care. But I remember it vividly.

There were many other times when I, like every mother, had to be separated from my young children. But you and I never have to be separated from our heavenly Father. We are never out of His sight.

"For the eyes of the Lord are on the righteous and his ears are attentive to their prayer" (1 Peter 3:12).

I, the God of Israel, will not forsake [you]. I will make rivers flow on barren heights, and springs within the valleys (Isaiah 41:17,18).

*L*ife has forced you to travel through unbelievably dry valleys. Your pain is intense. Your innermost being feels threatened. Your soul cries out, "God, why did You allow this to happen to me? How long must I endure this trial?" You thirst for a spring of hope. But God seems far away.

To a great extent, your life is shaped by how you respond to your valley experiences. In the valley of despair you may be tempted to close your heart to God's grace, doubting that He cares. But you can be sure He cares and that He will never forsake you.

Healing can begin while you are in the valley of despair. It was in my deepest, driest, loneliest valley that I discovered the most about God's love. My emotional pain became so great that I knew nothing mattered except God Himself. The valley cleared the way for God to reveal Himself to me in a new way. He became as real to me as life itself. His Word took on new life. I found that God is Lord of the valleys.

Even though I walk through the valley of the shadow of death, I will fear no evil, for you are with me (Psalm 23:4).

Valley experiences are inevitable. We all go through them at one time or another. No two valleys are alike. Some are long; some are short. Some are deeper than others. Some may be dark, causing great heartache and pain.

Your faith is tried in your valley experiences. You feel alone and forsaken. You wonder if you'll ever emerge from the valley. In one of her less-known hymns, the blind writer Fanny J. Crosby had words of encouragement for you when you're trudging through dark valleys:

> O child of God, wait patiently,
> When dark thy path may be;
> And let thy faith lean trustingly,
> On Him who cares for thee;
> And though the clouds hang drearily
> Upon the brow of night,
> Yet in the morning, joy will come
> And fill thy soul with light.

You're Never Alone

As the mountains surround Jerusalem, so the Lord surrounds his people both now and for-evermore" (Psalm 125:2).

*W*hen you feel all alone and God seems to be a million miles away, remind yourself that God's presence does not depend on your feelings, nor does His faithfulness depend on anything you do. It is the fact of His presence, not our sensation of His presence, that makes His presence real. Oswald Chambers says, "The *sense* of the presence is a super-added gift for which we give thanks when it comes."

You need never accept guilt for not feeling God's presence. Many others of our day and of previous centuries have had the same problem. For example, Jeanne Guyon, a saint of a writer who lived in the early eighteenth century, experienced a long period when she never felt the presence of God. Even when she read her Bible, she didn't feel His presence. She simply relied on what she knew in her heart to be truth.

Brother Lawrence was another saint who spoke of the discipline of the will. He wrote to a friend, "Let faith be your support. . . . Live in His Presence." He "surrounds" you.

3

When You're Fearful

The thief comes only to steal and kill and destroy; I have come that they may have life, and have it to the full (John 10:10).

*L*ouis XV, king of France, ordered that death was never to be spoken of in his presence. He avoided everything that reminded him of death. Obviously, the spiritual enemy had stolen the king's peace and replaced it with fear.

You may not fear death, as Louis XV did, but various circumstances may rob you of peace and joy. When you least expect them, moments of fear may overtake you. You feel as if there's no way out. Be assured that the Lord has prepared a way for you. He will still your anxious heart. Trust Him to show you the way and to lead you out of the darkness of fear into His marvelous light.

The voice of the enemy is always deceptive. Your dark enemy, Satan, would like to steal your joy, destroy your hope, and even take your life. But the Savior came to give His life so that you and I may have life to the full. He is stronger than any enemy we ever have to face. He alone is worthy of trust. Wait and trust. We will come through victoriously.

You're Never Alone

I sought the LORD, and he answered me; he delivered me from all my fears (Psalm 34:4).

*I*n the midst of his fears the psalmist knew where to turn. When you understand the marvelous love and grace of God, you too can find comfort in turning to Him when you feel alone and afraid. God's grace is as available to you as it was to the psalmist.

Fears and conflicts are all around us. We feel them in our own hearts because of what has gone on in our lives. But God is always present, waiting to deliver us from fear and fill us with His peace. Although it may not seem so, His peace and His presence are greater than our fears.

God's Word assures us that He has a purpose for us, and He will fulfill that purpose. God and His Word are our eternal hope. Meditating on His promises has been the only answer for me during my times of feeling fearful. He gave you and me His truth to enable us to go through times of fear, pressure, and conflict. Listening to His loving voice in Scripture as we read can carry us through an otherwise impossible situation. He is with us in every condition and circumstance.

You're Never Alone

Do not be afraid; do not be discouraged (Deuteronomy 1:21).

*S*ometimes you may feel as if you'll always be fearful and discouraged. You're not alone in your feelings. Even the Israelites of old felt that way. That's when the Lord told them not to be afraid or discouraged. At one point on their journey to the promised land, He informed them that they had stayed long enough where they were.

The Israelites made a fresh start and rebuilt their lives. The Lord loves you no less than He loved them. With His help, you can move on and rebuild your life. Making a new start always involves challenges. There are so many things to be afraid of. That's why the Lord says over and over in the Bible, "Do not be afraid."

"Do not be afraid" is an invitation to trust God by casting our cares on Him. When we learn to turn our focus from our seemingly hopeless condition to God and His love and power, our troubles and fears will fade away.

Too often other people disappoint us. But God never will. He is full of mercy and love. He promises never to leave us or forsake us, and He always keeps His promises.

You're Never Alone

The LORD will keep you from all harm—he will watch over your life (Psalm 121:7).

W hen you are in the midst of despair, you may be tempted to doubt if the Lord meant His promise to keep you from all harm. It may seem as if He has forgotten. Even the psalmist who proclaimed this truth had days when he felt weak and forsaken. He often made such cries as, "How long, O LORD? Will you forget me forever?" (Psalm 13:1). But he always recovered from his doubts and began to sing praises to God for His faithfulness.

You need not despair or condemn yourself for your doubts and fears. Remember that the greatest saints have had times when they felt weak and fearful. Our emotions are unstable. They often rise and fall according to our circumstances. God knows and understands without condemning us.

Our hopes must not be based on our state of mind or in what is going on around us, but in the person of Jesus Christ who loved us so much that He gave Himself for us. It is He who gives us joy and contentment. Turning our eyes from ourselves to Jesus helps us to remember His presence.

Whoever touches you touches the apple of his eye (Zechariah 2:8).

*I*f I had been deeply aware that I am as dear to God as the pupil of His eye, I could have relaxed during those times when I was steeped in fear. I had read that Scripture often, but I had not grasped the depth of its meaning.

Unfortunately, most of us focus our eyes not on God and His all-consuming love for us, but upon our fears. We are tempted to dread and fear when circumstances seem to go against us. Our problems look like giants, while we feel like grasshoppers in comparison.

It doesn't matter how great your problems are; God is greater. God never will allow your problems to become so great that they overwhelm you. You may sometimes *feel* overwhelmed. But God always has a way out for you.

It may be difficult to let go of your fears and trust God completely. Even the apostles, after living with Jesus for three years, found it difficult not to be afraid. Like us, they often became riddled with doubts. But as Jesus helped them through such times, He will also help you.

You're Never Alone

Fear not [there is nothing to fear], for I am with you; do not look around you in terror and be dismayed, for I am your God (Isaiah 41:10 AMP).

I woke up in the night, fearful of what was going on. I followed our usual human tendency to focus on the problem, rather than focusing my attention on the Lord. I turned on the light, picked up my Bible from the bedside table, and read the above verse.

"Nothing to fear? Lord, are You sure?" I inwardly questioned. Then I noticed He said "for I am with you." Of course, if He were with me in the flesh, I would not be afraid. But it is often so difficult to realize His presence in spirit. Such trust requires faith. I could only pray, "Lord, I *want* to believe. Help me to trust You more completely."

I closed my Bible, turned out the light, and meditated on the verse until my mind was filled with peace and I fell asleep. A few days later I read author Phillip Keller's suggestion that when our lives are linked with God, "even the dark and difficult times are not seen as disasters, but as disciplines that lead to greater goals."

The LᵉᵣḴ watches over you—the LᵉᵣḴ is your shade at your right hand. . . . The LᵉᵣḴ will keep you from all harm—he will watch over your life (Psalm 121:5,7).

God's loving presence is illustrated in the way the American Indians trained their young braves. After a boy had faced various trials in hunting and fishing with his father, he was ready for the final test. Late in the evening he was blindfolded and led into a dense, dark forest to spend the night alone.

Too terrified even to consider going to sleep, the boy wondered if the night would ever end. Every noise, gust of wind, or snap of a twig was magnified, suggesting the approach of a ferocious, hungry animal.

At last the sun's rays filtering through the trees penetrated the blindfold sufficiently to inform the boy that morning had come. Slipping the cover from his eyes, the boy was astonished to see his father only a few feet away. The father had been there all night, keeping watch over his son.

When we feel that we're alone in a dense, dark forest, we can be sure that our heavenly Father is watching over us.

4

*When You Feel
Trapped*

*The eyes of the L*ORD *are on the righteous and his ears are attentive to their cry* (Psalm 34:15).

"Lord, stop the world! I want to get off." Life had become too much for a friend of mine. She went into the woods and cried to the Lord to let her get off the whirling world. As far as she was concerned, the Lord did let her off the world that day. He gave her the strong assurance that He was with her and that she could release all her problems to Him.

God doesn't often remove us from our painful situations. He does hear our cry, come into our situations with us, and give us the wisdom and strength to bear our loads. Or He reminds us to release our problems to Him.

By leaving you in your situation and being with you in the midst of it, He is able to give you a greater vision of His goodness and power. His eyes are always upon you. He never fails to hear your cry for help. He may not answer in the way you expect. But you can be assured He knows what is best for you and will provide.

He will lead you into the perfect plan He has for you. You are never alone.

You're Never Alone

For the LORD comforts his people and will have compassion on his afflicted ones (Isaiah 49:13).

*R*egardless of how bad you feel or how negative the events are in your life, God loves you. He has compassion for you. He delights to comfort you. He who created all things listens when you pray. He sees you whether you're out for a walk, in bed, hardly able to move, or going about your daily duties. That is a part of His comfort and compassion.

When you have been hurt and disappointed, you may forget who you are: a child of the King of the universe. He has created all things for your enjoyment and healing. You may find a certain degree of healing simply from concentrating on the beauty around you. Look at all the things God has freely provided for your enjoyment.

Take time to enjoy the *taste* of a fresh slice of buttered bread. *Smell* the fragrance of a cake baking in the oven. *Feel* the cool breeze in your face when you go for a walk. *Touch* a flower petal and be reminded that God created it for your enjoyment. *Listen* to the birds singing on a quiet morning. *See* what God has done for you.

Blessed is the man who trusts in the L̥ord, whose confidence is in him (Jeremiah 17:7).

*W*ill Rogers said, "People who fly into a rage always make a bad landing." Publicus Syrus declared, "An angry man is again angry at himself when he returns to reason."

Are you trapped by anger at God because of childhood hurts—hurts which still haunt you? God understands and loves you nonetheless. In moments of anger or fear, you may feel unworthy of God's love. Through Jesus you are worthy. You need not be angry at yourself for your angry feelings toward God. He loves you unconditionally. He is as much with you when you feel trapped in an unpleasant situation as He is when you feel His liberating presence.

As you begin to see God's true nature, a weight lifts from your shoulders. You will know that God's purpose is to heal your hurts, never to vent His anger against you. When you learn to view yourself from His perspective, you will feel better about yourself. You can always trust Him and put your confidence in Him.

"Then you will know the truth, and the truth will set you free" (John 8:32). Knowing and believing the truth offers you hope and confidence as nothing else can.

You're Never Alone

My help comes from the Lᴏʀᴅ, the Maker of heaven and earth (Psalm 121:2).

Sometimes you feel like standing in the middle of the street and yelling, "Help!" But no one answers your cry. You doubt whether anyone cares. You wonder if your life is so badly messed up that you're trapped forever.

You are not alone in your feelings. Many have felt that way. Neither are you alone as far as God is concerned. He is your ever-present Helper and the Lover of your soul.

The Maker of heaven and earth is never too busy for you. You can tell Him every detail of your life and know that He is listening. *Why doesn't He hurry and answer or change my situation?* you ask. *Why must I continue feeling trapped?*

You are making progress. Spiritual growth and healing are processes. God is at work in your behalf even when you are not aware of anything changing.

Remember, you are victorious through Jesus. He will not fail you. He desires your well-being. Lean on Him and wait expectantly. Your help is in Him.

The Lord knows how to rescue godly men [and women] from trials (2 Peter 2:9).

*O*ur trials arrive in different vehicles. But by whatever means they come, trials are a part of living in our fallen world. Sooner or later, trials invade every life and often make us feel trapped. Trials hurt. Your trials probably seem worse than mine to you; mine seem worse than yours to me.

God does not send the trials in which we seem to be trapped. He may allow them. But because of His great love for us, His desire is to deliver us out of them. His purpose is to mend our brokenness and make us whole.

God often uses our trials to chip away the rough edges in our character. Job said concerning his trials: "When he has tested me, I will come forth as gold" (Job 23:10). Job obviously understood what Paul said hundreds of years later: God predetermined that we should be conformed to the image of His Son (Romans 8:29). Trials help to accomplish that.

If we can view our trials in the light of what God can do with them in our behalf and for His glory, God will give us courage to bear them until He delivers us out of them.

When I was in distress, I sought the Lord; at night I stretched out untiring hands and my soul refused to be comforted (Psalm 77:2).

*H*ave you ever felt as David did? You sought the Lord, but still your soul refused to be comforted? Most of us have had such experiences. When we feel trapped in an unpleasant situation, we may seek the Lord but find no immediate comfort. The lack is not on God's part, of course. It is our feeling of despair that often keeps us from being aware of His presence or His answer.

All of us encounter rough places in life. But our all-wise God would remind us that He has His hand upon our lives. He is preparing us for something in the future. He says, "Don't give up. Trust me. Victory is closer than you think."

Feeling trapped makes it difficult for us to remember that God has a hand in our lives. But His Word assures us again and again that God indeed has a plan and a purpose for each of us. He is aware of every issue we face, small or great, and He cares.

Believing that God cares requires faith. "Faith is our gaze upon a saving God," wrote minister/author

A.W. Tozer. "It is not a one-time act, but a continuous gaze."

5

When You Feel Weak

The LORD upholds all those who fall and lifts up all who are bowed down (Psalm 145:14).

arly in the life of a young midwestern lawyer, he wrote, "I am the most miserable man living. Whether I shall ever recover, I cannot tell." He did recover and rose to become one of America's most beloved presidents—Abraham Lincoln.

Sometimes you feel so weak and helpless that you wonder if there's any reason for hope. The Lord seems far away. Be assured in those moments that the Lord is as near you and as much *for* you as in those times when you feel His loving presence. He promises never to leave you or forsake you.

His love is constant. Nothing can stop His enfolding you in His love. Your inner pain and feeling of weakness keep you from being aware of His loving presence. Do not be anxious. He is present to gently support you in your times of weakness. He delights to prove His loving care for His weak, discouraged children.

"The eyes of the LORD are on those who fear him, on those whose hope is in his unfailing love" (Psalm 33:18). Be assured that His eyes are always upon you for your good.

49

I have set before you life and death, blessings and curses. Now choose life, so that you . . . may live (Deuteronomy 30:19).

Recently I read Lloyd Ogilvie's book *God Believes in You*. In my moments of weakness I may doubt whether God believes in me. But I can *choose* to believe it and be blessed. I may not find my circumstances immediately changing, but my attitude changes, and I trust God more completely. His life becomes more abundant in me.

Life is filled with choices. In previous years many of your choices were made for you. You had no control over what happened. On many occasions you were the victim of circumstance. No longer does that have to be true. God is at work in you. He lives within you to empower you to change your life. But He leaves the choice to you.

God created you with a free will. You can be bound by the weaknesses of your past, or you can leave your past behind. Refuse to dwell on unhappy memories. God calls you to move on to higher things and live in His joy and peace. He has a joyful purpose for your life. On the cross Jesus bore your weaknesses along with your sins. In our times of weakness, we can cry out to Him for help.

He tends his flock like a shepherd: He gathers the lambs in his arms and carries them close to his heart; he gently leads those that have young (Isaiah 40:11).

Many times in both the Old and New Testaments the Lord pictures His loving care by comparing it to the gentleness of a good shepherd. God is gentle and loving, yet firm and strong.

The purpose of God's message is to strengthen, comfort, and bless. He will never give up on you. When you are weakest, He carries you in His arms like a good shepherd carries his lambs. You are always close to the heart of God. Incredible as it may seem to you, you are never out of His thoughts. That's how great His love is for you.

In your weakness, you may have strayed away from God. He patiently waits for your return. He will restore your love relationship with Him. Regardless of how weak you may be, God desires fellowship with you because He loves you. You are one of His precious and valuable sheep. God is not looking for perfect people to serve Him. He is looking for those who will allow Him to lead them.

You're Never Alone

You may be overtaken by feelings of weakness.
The song in your heart may have forsaken you, but
you are not alone.

You're Never Alone

Be strong and courageous. Do not be terrified;
*do not be discouraged, for the L*O*RD your God*
will be with you wherever you go (Joshua 1:9).

*T*he Lord knows you cannot be strong and
courageous on your own. He is pleased when
you surrender totally to Him and admit your weaknesses. Only then can He infuse you with His
strength.

Problems have the power to make us or break
us. Without the strength that God provides, they are
sure to break the strongest of us. With His help,
troubles can make us stronger than we could have
been without their occurrence. It is in the midst of
life's perplexities that God manifests His strength in
our behalf.

The only problems that can defeat us are those
we try to handle without God's help. Sometimes in
our impatience we may want to help God out or
speed things up. That never works out for our good
or anyone else's. God will give us strength to
endure while we wait.

He reminds us, "Do not be discouraged. You are
not alone. I am with you to provide strength for
your weakness every moment of every day."

Therefore, if anyone is in Christ, he is a new creation; the old has gone, the new has come! (2 Corinthians 5:17).

*J*oseph received a coat of many colors from his father, Jacob. The coat symbolized Jacob's love for and approval of his son. In the spiritual realm, you have received a coat of many colors. God's smile of love and approval is upon you, never to be removed. He has made you His beloved child. His strength is your strength.

When you have been rejected or put down by loved ones, you may feel as if nothing ever will be right. You know you have accepted Christ and that you belong to Him, but everything seems to be wrong inside you. You feel helplessly weak. Old thoughts cling to you, and you feel that you must derive your identity from the past.

We have to learn not to allow others to tell us who we are. When we accept Christ as Savior and Lord, we receive our identity from Him. Whether we feel like it or not, we are new creatures in Him. Renewing our mind by reading and meditating on uplifting passages of Scripture helps us to realize who we are: new creatures, beloved children of God.

The spirit is willing, but the body is weak
(Matthew 26:41).

*J*esus spoke the above words to His three closest friends. They had fallen asleep at the time when He most needed their support. Facing the cross, Jesus felt sorrowful and troubled as He prayed alone in the Garden of Gethsemane. Yet, He did not condemn His friends for their weakness in falling sleep. He realized their bodily limitations.

For various reasons, you and I often find ourselves weak and helpless at the very times we would like to be alert. We may feel alone and ashamed in our weakness. We can be comforted by the thought that Jesus understands and does not condemn us.

The apostle Paul said, "When I am weak, then I am strong" (2 Corinthians 12:10). He meant, of course, that it was not his own strength that availed but the strength of Christ. So it is with us. Our human strength—spiritual, emotional, and physical—knows limitations. But the strength of our Lord is sufficient in every situation. And even in our weakness, our heavenly Father takes pleasure in us. We are not alone.

You're Never Alone

Great are the works of the LORD; they are pondered by all who delight in them (Psalm 111:2).

A man walking down the street, feeling weak and half-dead, stopped in his tracks when he saw a sign in the window of a funeral home. The sign read, "Why walk around half-dead? We can bury you for a few hundred dollars. P.S. We give green stamps." The humor of the words jolted him out of his feeling of weakness.

When we know that we have God on our side and yet we feel weak, we need something to jolt us out of our weak feelings. It may be that we need to take some time for self-nurturing. Maybe we need to do as the psalmists obviously did—ponder the works of the Lord. The beauty of His creation is meant to nurture our souls.

If we take time to ponder the beauty of God's creation, we find He can use that as a means of nurturing us and bringing us out of our feelings of weakness. I glean strength by taking a few minutes to revel in the hues of the eastern sky just before sunrise, to glimpse God's beauty in the variety of magnificent colors of flowers, and to listen to the sounds of nature. It was for God's pleasure and ours that He created all things.

That is why, for Christ's sake, I delight in weaknesses, in insults, in hardships, in persecutions, in difficulties. For when I am weak, then I am strong (2 Corinthians 12:10).

*T*he apostle Paul realized, as perhaps no other person ever has, that in himself he was weak but that Christ's power was sufficient for him. He refused to allow his weakness to hinder him. In his ministry, Paul suffered hardships and pressures almost beyond endurance (see 1 Corinthians 1:8). Yet, Paul knew that his strength was in the Lord.

A missionary to China in the 1880s, J. Hudson Taylor often struggled to overcome discouragement and depression. During his early years in China, he lost his wife and two of their young children to diseases of the hot summer. He learned that in his own strength he could do nothing. But he found the Lord to be the Source of his strength.

Hudson Taylor once wrote that his work had never been so hard, "but the weight and strain are all gone." He learned to accept his weakness and let God be strong in him. He said, "All God's giants have been weak men, who did great things for God

because they reckoned on His being with them."
Hudson Taylor knew he was not alone.

6

When You're Depressed

The LORD is a refuge for the oppressed, a stronghold in times of trouble (Psalm 9:9).

*A*ctress Mary Martin was facing a trying situation. One night at curtain time, she wondered if she could go onstage. Just then someone handed her a note of encouragement. That note enabled her to give a fine performance.

Are you oppressed because of the circumstances in your life? Are you wondering if you can go on? The Lord has handed you a note of encouragement in His Word and by His Spirit. He invites you to lean on Him. He is ready to lead you out of depression and restore you to emotional health.

The Lord wants His presence to be like a warm blanket, reminding you of His nearness and of how much He cares for you. He desires that you feel the warmth of His love enfolding you, even as a young eagle feels the warmth of its mother's feathers sheltering it from harm.

His presence can be your comfort during these days of recovery to emotional wholeness. Let His peace fill your heart, giving you hope for tomorrow. Receive His note of encouragement.

"Though the mountains be shaken and the hills be removed, yet my unfailing love for you will not be shaken nor my covenant of peace be removed," says the LORD, who has compassion on you (Isaiah 54:10).

*H*ow easily we fall into doubting God's loving care when everything in life seems to go against us. It happens to the greatest of saints. The man who wrote the inspiring hymn "Come Thou Fount" experienced just such a down time many years after writing the hymn which has blessed many.

One day a stranger asked him if he knew the hymn. Through tears, he replied, "I am the unhappy man who wrote the hymn. I'd give anything to have those feelings again."

None of us is exempt from times of discouragement and depression. But the Lord reminds us in His Word that regardless of what may happen around us, His unfailing love will not be shaken. Troubles do not last forever for God's children. His love does. He invites you to keep your eyes on Him. You can be assured that He is a God of peace and compassion. He will renew your hope and restore your peace and joy.

"Cast all your anxiety on him because he cares for you" (1 Peter 5:7).

Do not be afraid, for I am with you (Isaiah 43:5).

A man temporarily blinded by tears of grief wrote, "My palace of dreams has collapsed, but I am building a cathedral out of the ruins."

You may feel that you're going through the worst trial of your life. God's purpose is not to destroy you but to conform you to the image of His Son. He will help you take the ruins of your life and "build a cathedral" for His glory and for your blessing.

God does not cause your depression. But He is with you in it. He is aware of you. He knows your every need. Even when you feel alone, God is present with you.

Your spiritual enemy would like to deceive you and cause you to doubt God's love and presence. Never listen to a voice that casts doubt on the goodness of God. God is always for you. He will help you.

God never speaks a message of fear or hopelessness. He *corrects*, but He never condemns His children. God always offers love, peace, hope, and joy. He offers only that which accords with His nature. He is with you to help you. He has promised to be with you and guide you. He will keep His promise to you.

He predestined us to be adopted as his sons through Jesus Christ, in accordance with his pleasure and will (Ephesians 1:5).

Things have happened to make you feel like a nobody. Your self-confidence stands at zero. You're so depressed that you feel there's nothing worthwhile you can do. But when you fully realize you have been adopted by a loving heavenly Father, your self-confidence will start to soar.

The reformer Ulrich Zwingli said our confidence in Christ "urges us on and makes us active in living righteous lives." The Lord restores your lost self-confidence and empowers you to be all He created you to be.

The Lord has rescued you from the dominion of darkness and transferred you into His kingdom of light. When you put your trust in Him, He shares His righteousness with you, whether you feel worthy of righteousness or not.

Paul wrote to the Christians of Rome saying, "To all in Rome who are loved by God and called to be saints..." If you have accepted His salvation, His words apply not only to the Roman Christians but also to you. He calls you a saint. Give Him your depression. Rejoice. He is with you.

Those who hope in me will not be disappointed
(Isaiah 49:23).

*M*illions of dollars have been spent to build magnificent bridges. The Tacoma Narrows suspension bridge swayed violently in stormy winds in 1940 and collapsed. Other bridges also have failed and disappointed people.

The Lord is the Bridge between your depression and your release. He is the Bridge that will never disappoint you. You can trust Him completely. No stormy winds in your life can ever destroy the bridge of His faithfulness to you.

When you're so depressed that you can see no way out of your difficult situation, Jesus points you to Himself—your Bridge of safety. Instead of focusing on your feelings of despair, focus on the Lord.

God never causes adversity. But He may use adversity to lead you into greater spiritual blessings than you could receive in any other way. Ask Him to give you wisdom to deal with the difficulty you're going through. God has an overall plan for your life. See yourself as He sees you—as His beloved child. He will never disappoint you. Press on along the upward path until you gain new heights. Make higher ground your aim.

You're Never Alone

Come to me, all you who are weary and burdened, and I will give you rest (Matthew 11:28).

Some people think that spiritually committed Christians should never become depressed. Nothing could be further from the truth. The intensity of a person's emotional suffering is often in direct proportion to his/her devotion to God. David, whom God described as a man after His own heart, often cried out to God with such words as, "I am worn out calling for help; my throat is parched. My eyes fail, looking for my God" (Psalm 69:3).

Some time ago a friend came to me and said, "I lost all the ground I'd gained when I lost my temper yesterday." Intent on rapid spiritual growth, she felt depressed by her obvious setback.

All of us experience what Vance Havner called three levels: "mountaintop days" when everything seems rosy, "ordinary days" when we are neither elated nor depressed, and "dark days" when we feel that our world is caving in on us. Through them all, we can rest in the assurance that we are not alone. God is with us.

Depression can lead us to know the Lord more fully than ever before as we look to Him for help and encouragement.

7

When You Feel
Like a Failure

He calls his own sheep by name and leads them out (John 10:3).

*J*ust as the shepherds of Eastern culture called each of their sheep by name, the Lord knows your name. He not only knows your name, He knows your personality, your needs, and all about you. He even knows all your faults and weaknesses and still loves you.

At night, shepherds of Bible times led their sheep to an area protected on three sides by rocks or shrubs. Then the shepherds lay down and slept in the open space, literally becoming the gate to the sheepfold. In this way they protected their sheep from any possible dangers.

In a spiritual sense the Lord does the same thing for you and me. He sacrificed His life so that we might be victorious over our problems. He knows that we may keep failing, but He calls us by name, back to the way He knows is best for us.

God is able to use our mistakes and the mistakes of those who have hurt us. In so doing, He brings about our ultimate good. In Him we can find security. He is closer to us than our own breath.

I am he who will sustain you. I have made you and I will carry you; I will sustain you and I will rescue you (Isaiah 46:4).

When God says He will sustain you, He means He will care for you and provide for you. He will rescue you from all danger. He is the everlasting, sovereign God who does what He promises. Why will He do this for unworthy persons like you and me? We are valuable to Him. He loves us. He sees worth in us that neither we nor anyone else can see.

Other people may put you down and tell you in words or actions that you're a failure. Never listen to anything contrary to what God says. You receive your identity not from friends or family or strangers but from God.

God has made you a new creature in Christ. Regardless of what has come in your life to make you feel like an unworthy failure, God still says, "I have made you and I will restore you." He will be your God throughout your life to carry you through whatever difficult times you may face. He does not see you as a failure but as His beloved child.

"Come now, let us reason together," says the LORD. "Though your sins are like scarlet, they shall be as white as snow; though they are red as crimson, they shall be like wool" (Isaiah 1:18).

I've done it again," my friend wrote. "I'm so discouraged when I realize I keep repeating the same sin over and over. I'm embarrassed to come before God. I don't feel worthy to ask again for forgiveness."

My friend reminds me of several others who brood over their failures before they grasp the graciousness of God. Heaviness hangs like a black cloud over their souls. Until your spirit grasps the truth of the Word, you remain in despair.

The good news is that the crushing weight of condemnation melts away when your spirit encounters the truth that God is waiting to wash away your sins and make you "white as snow."

Regardless of how many times you may have failed God, yourself, or other people, His grace is always the same. His love never wavers. His greatness fills heaven and earth. He loves you more than you can ever imagine. You need never feel that you should hide behind a facade in God's presence. He loves you and is with you in your failures.

Let every man learn to assess properly the value of his own work and he can then be glad when he has done something worth doing without depending on the approval of others (Galatians 6:4, PHILLIPS).

*O*ne of our greatest needs is a proper evaluation of ourselves and what we do. Many of us judge ourselves or compare ourselves unfavorably with other people. Then we become impatient with ourselves or put ourselves down. No two of us are exactly alike. God made us all unique. He likes variety.

To know our value is not prideful. Having a strong sense of who we are in Christ is healthy. We have purpose. When we know how valuable we are in God's sight, we don't have to spend time looking for the approval of others. We know that no one else can duplicate us.

You are of special value to God because you are His. When other people hurt you or criticize you, you can be sure that their hurts or criticisms are not of God. He is for you. God has promised never to leave you or reject you in any way. Enjoy knowing your value and the value of your work.

You're Never Alone

Find what gives you pleasure in your alone times. If it honors the Lord, give yourself to it.

You will again have compassion on us; you will tread our sins underfoot and hurl all our iniquities into the depths of the sea (Micah 7:19).

God is always compassionate toward His children when they seek to do His will. You need not wallow in guilt over sins God has forgiven. His Word assures us that if we confess our sins, He forgives and blots them out of His remembrance. Condemning yourself only prolongs your pain.

Clouds hanging over your head can serve to remind you to walk by faith. Clouds of doubt may make you feel that something is wrong with you. Remember, you are still growing. You are God's child and you are His responsibility. Refuse to dwell on any dark clouds from your past. Do not allow anything of your past or present to weigh you down.

When clouds of doubt engulf you, look upon them in the full assurance that God is with you. Never permit even the darkest clouds to affect your faith in what God is doing in your life. He will not leave you. He is always for you. You are His to care for. He will never give up on you. Keep trusting Him. You will see His answer.

[God] is above and greater than our consciences (our hearts), and He knows (perceives and understands) everything [nothing is hidden from Him] (1 John 3:20 AMP).

Sometimes either our consciences or our spiritual enemy make us feel like we are failures. But we are in God's hands. We need not listen to accusations from our consciences or from any enemy—on the inside or on the outside.

God is not fretting about our weaknesses. He knows it takes time for us to grow, just as it takes time for an apple on a tree to mature. We can trust Him to bring us to greater strength and maturity.

God is greater than anything we fear concerning ourselves, our growth, or our future. The outcome is already settled as far as He is concerned. We are free to rest in Him and His ability to strengthen us.

Let us remember that God loves us without regard to our performance. As Dr. Charles Stanley says, God's part in the believer's life is unconditional love. Our part is unconditional trust in Him.

Be joyful in hope, patient in affliction, faithful in prayer (Romans 12:12).

A certain man of the past century could have easily given in to feelings of failure. But he remained "joyful in hope." More than once he failed in business. In 1832 he ran for the legislature and was defeated.

Three times he ran for Congress and suffered defeat each time. Twice he was defeated for the Senate, and once for vice president. But he refused to accept failure as his destiny. In 1860 he was elected the sixteenth president of the United States. Four years later, he was reelected. Today we remember Abraham Lincoln as one of the finest Christian leaders the United States has ever had.

One of the greatest qualities God has given us as His children is the ability to persevere in spite of obvious failure. Regardless of what has happened in our past or may be happening now, God is able to redeem it. God is able to use and turn into good anything we may perceive as a failure. "Doubt sees the obstacles. Faith sees the way! Doubt sees the darkest night. Faith sees the day. Doubt dreads to take a step. Faith soars on high" (Anonymous).

8

When You Feel Hopeless

Don't let the world around you squeeze you into its own mold, but let God remold your minds from within, so that you may prove in practice that the plan of God for you is good (Romans 12:2, PHILLIPS).

The world around you will try to shape your mind and squeeze you into its mold. The world may tell you that your situation is hopeless, that you may as well give up. But the world does not know God and His ways. Never listen to what those outside of Christ tell you. God is a God of love and mercy. He never writes His children off as hopeless.

God's plan for you is good. He has chosen to deliver you from all the ill effects of your past. You can trust Him. The world may tell you that you are doomed to a meaningless life. God's intention is to deliver you from a life of meaninglessness and purposelessness to a life overflowing with meaning and purpose. You can always trust God's intentions.

"He who did not spare his own Son, but gave him up for us all—how will he not also, along with him, graciously give us all things?" (Romans 8:32).

You come to the help of those who gladly do right, who remember your ways (Isaiah 64:5).

Nothing can distract the guards who stand outside Buckingham Palace. They are intent on one thing only: protecting the palace and everyone and everything in it or surrounding it.

The Lord Himself is more intent than that on caring for you. Everything that concerns you concerns Him. That's how much He loves you. When you realize that He is your source of help and call upon Him, He will come to your aid.

God has various ways of helping His hurting children. He may choose to support you through other people. God often uses His mature, caring children to be channels of His healing love and to represent Himself. He may lead you to a new friend, to a group, or to a certain book or tape with a hopeful message.

The way out of feelings of hopelessness is sometimes a slow journey. Never let the slowness cause you to doubt God's faithfulness. You can always count on Him. He has chosen to heal and bless His children. He will never let you down. His promises are as sure as His Word.

One thing I do: Forgetting what is behind and straining toward what is ahead, I press on (Philippians 3:13).

A man broke into Tania's house and assaulted her. The trauma was so great that she moved to another town. But Tania couldn't shake the horrible memories.

Six months later she went to a counselor, saying she couldn't separate herself from the experience. "I'm sure I'll remain hopeless the rest of my life," she declared.

The counselor explained that even though she had been the victim of an ugly tragedy, she could get over her feelings of hopelessness resulting from victimization and realize she was no less a child of God.

With God's help, Tania finally put the trauma behind her and saw her past in the light of what Christ had done for her at the cross. She realized that she still belonged to Him. Instead of feeling hopeless, she could grow and be of help to others as a result of her unfortunate experience.

All of us have had experiences that left us emotionally scarred. We need not allow our past circumstances to make us feel hopeless. God can turn them around for our good and His glory.

My grace is sufficient for you, for my power is made perfect in weakness (2 Corinthians 12:9).

*E*very day may be viewed as a book with blank pages. The Lord promises to publish it. What we include on those pages is up to us. The nature of our "writing" depends on our response to circumstances. Many of our circumstances are beyond our control. Life's happenings often are events we never would choose if we were given a choice.

Life does not come without conflict. As much as we would like to avoid it, spiritual warfare must be expected. Oswald Chambers made this strange statement: "The saint never knows the joy of the Lord in spite of tribulation, but because of it." When we face hardships and feelings of hopelessness, we can be sure the Lord is at work in our lives for a good purpose.

The Lord promises never to leave us or forsake us. He loves us too much to leave us to ourselves. He never requires us to fight our battles alone. Regardless of how we feel—hopeless or beyond redemption—we can be assured that God's grace is sufficient. He never sees us as hopeless. He can lift us up and make us like new.

It is God who works in you to will and to act according to his good purpose (Philippians 2:13).

A little black boy stood watching while a man filled balloons of several different colors and released them into the air. Finally, the little boy gathered the courage to ask, "If you filled a black balloon, would it go up, too?"

"Sure," the man replied. "It's not the color of the balloon that counts. It's what's inside."

Sometimes you feel so hopeless that you wonder if you have inside what it takes to rise above your situation. If you have the Lord, you have all it takes. He has promised to be with you at all times.

You can rest in the assurance that your feeling of hopelessness and inner pain is temporary. The Lord often works more slowly than we would like. But He knows best. He alone knows how much spiritual surgery we can stand at any given time.

The steadfast love of the Lord never fails. He has set His eternal seal of love upon you. Remember, He loves you personally and unconditionally. He will supply you with what it takes to rise above your situation. He never leaves you alone.

Why are you downcast, O my soul? Why so disturbed within me? Put your hope in God, for I will yet praise him, my Savior and my God (Psalm 42:5).

*T*he psalmist knew where to turn when he felt hopeless and downcast. He knew that God alone could lift him up when he felt discouraged. David's God is our God. He has that same unconditional love for us that He had for David.

God's desire for all His children is that we rejoice in Him and in His goodness and grace, instead of fretting over our seeming hopelessness.

When feelings of hopelessness set in, we feel as if all our future days will be days of gloom, that the sun will never shine again. I've been there. I've had to remind myself again and again that no matter how dark the skies may appear, the sun will shine again.

God is for us. He is with us. He will never let us down. He says, "I will not in any way... leave you helpless nor forsake you nor let [you] down" (Hebrews 13:5 AMP). We can always depend on His Word. He never violates His promises.

9

*When You've Been
Ill-Treated*

You shall no longer be termed Forsaken, nor shall your land any more be termed Desolate. ... For the LORD delights in you (Isaiah 62:4,5 NKJV).

*G*od promised a magnificent restoration to Jerusalem. The city, which had been degraded and abused by conquerors, would be rebuilt and restored.

Whether you have been abused by parents, spouse, other family members, friends, or strangers, or if your pain has been self-inflicted, God's desire is to rebuild your life and bring restoration to you just as He did for Jerusalem.

Regardless of what may have happened in your past or what may be going on now, the Lord wants you never to feel desolate or forsaken. Simply because He created you and you belong to Him, He delights in you and wants to restore your joy.

When Jesus walked on this earth in His physical body, His attention always seemed to be focused on the person in greatest need. He delights in restoring joy and gladness to those who have been forsaken. He knows and cares when you need His healing touch.

You're Never Alone

The LORD's unfailing love surrounds the [person] who trusts in him (Psalm 32:10).

*S*everal years ago when a crisis struck my life, I felt as if every anchor to which I had clung had been removed. *If only this had not happened, everything would be all right,* I told myself. I mistakenly had put my trust in a human being instead of in the Lord. My cycle of loneliness continued until I allowed the Lord to break the cycle.

I had to realize that the Lord alone can satisfy the heart's desire for wholeness. His unfailing love was surrounding me, but I had to recognize His presence before I could receive His joy and peace.

When we turn to God to satisfy our emptiness, He never disappoints us. He longs to spend time with us, heal our brokenness, and fulfill us in ways we never dreamed possible.

The wonder of God's love is that He gives us more than things. His love is more than a warm feeling, more than providing materially for us. He gives us Himself. He gives us all of Himself so that we can be all that He has planned for us to be. He simply asks that we *receive* His love.

I have seen his ways, but I will heal him; I will guide him and restore comfort to him (Isaiah 57:18).

*T*he pain in your life may have been so great that it led you to resort to habits you now regret. Such negative patterns are difficult to break. They cause you to feel miserable and helplessly guilty. You may feel unworthy to call upon God.

But our ever-loving Father sees, understands, and forgives. Condemnation is not a part of His nature. He knows what happened to drive you to the state you're in. He is present to guide you out of your condition. He will help you overcome whatever is binding you. He has promised to heal you and restore comfort to your soul.

God not only forgives. He also enables you to forgive those who have hurt you and whom you feel are responsible for your unhappiness. When you feel the most ill-treated, God may become the most real. He can reveal new truths to you—truths you might have missed without your dark experiences. Nothing is too dark for God to shine His love upon and change—in ways you never dreamed possible. He has healing ways beyond your wildest imagination.

His divine power has given us everything we need for life and godliness through our knowledge of him who called us by his own glory and goodness (2 Peter 1:3).

*H*ow helpless we feel when life has hit us with cruel blows. But how comforting to know that through Christ we possess everything we need to rebuild our lives and live fully and meaningfully. The more we grow in our knowledge of Him, the more we understand that He has called us to be fulfilled in Him.

We cannot undo our past, but with God's help we can change its effect on us. By surrendering our future to God, we can rest in the assurance that He will supply all we need to become what He created us to be. That's His promise.

Today is filled with opportunities to grow in our knowledge of God and in understanding more of His love and kindness. God is a God of goodness and grace. As a good parent always provides the best he can for his children, God more than provides His best for His children. God's provision includes help to rise above our circumstances so we are no longer controlled by them.

In God I trust; I will not be afraid. What can [people] do to me? (Psalm 56:11).

*P*eople constantly let us down. At least it seems so. Our problem is that we allow the punitive attitudes that others express toward us to fill us with self-doubt and fear. And our fragile self-concept is damaged. The bigger danger is that we may allow other voices to distort the sound of God's loving voice. We especially tend to equate God with those whom we regard as authority figures.

The psalmist learned not to allow other people to influence His life. You, too, can learn to trust God completely. As you practice tuning out the words spoken by those who have hurt you or made you feel put down, you will build a new self-concept based on God's unconditional love. You never have to yield to negative feelings that others may have tried to force upon you. God has decided in your favor.

"Therefore, there is now no condemnation for those who are in Christ Jesus" (Romans 8:1). Since that is true, we need not allow others to heap guilt upon us. God is for us. He is ready to help us rid ourselves of hurts due to being ill-treated. He is always present to bless us.

He was despised and rejected by men, a man of sorrows, and familiar with suffering (Isaiah 53:3).

No one ever has or ever will suffer the ill treatment that our Savior endured. It is impossible for any of us to be acquainted with grief in the way our Lord was. Jesus came and endured grief in every form in order to set us free.

That doesn't mean that we're exempt from suffering, sorrow, and ill treatment. It does mean God is with us in our pain. He understands and bears it with us. Painful memories of what life has done to us may come to haunt us. But as someone suggested, we need not build a monument to the ugly memory.

We have the choice of wasting a portion of our lives by clutching old memories or of using our past as motivation for future growth. God is able to use our every experience for God. The working out of everything for our good comprises a large part of His business as our loving, all-powerful Father. That is a large part of His business as our loving, all-powerful Father.

Life's ill treatments are opportunities for us to allow God to show Himself strong in our behalf.

10

*When Divorce
Strikes*

Never will I leave you; never will I forsake you (Hebrews 13:5).

When my friend's husband deserted her, she felt like a child alone in a dense, dark forest. Her world was filled with loneliness and pain. Her night of sorrow looked unending. Our experiences are different, but not one of us is exempt from times of distress. Hurt is a part of life.

In spite of what we experience or how we feel, we can rest assured that morning will come. We are never alone. We have a Friend who is always with us. His promises are as sure as His creation. He watches over us to care for us.

" 'Though the mountains be shaken and the hills be removed, yet my unfailing love for you will not be shaken nor my covenant of peace be removed,' says the LORD, who has compassion on you" (Isaiah 54:10).

As surely as we walk through valleys of discouragement and pain, just as surely we will emerge victoriously on the other side. God never allows His children to remain in their troubles. We can affirm with the psalmist David, "The LORD is my light and my salvation—whom shall I fear?" (Psalm 27:1).

I have loved you with an everlasting love; I have drawn you with loving-kindness (Jeremiah 31:3).

When we feel especially lonely and in need of great love, we can find peace in knowing that the God who is greater than any circumstance knows and cares. God, the Father of love, loves us with an everlasting love. He knows how we feel. His Father-heart is touched with our every grief.

He has promised to "provide for those who grieve in Zion—to bestow on them a crown of beauty instead of ashes, the oil of gladness instead of mourning, and a garment of praise instead of a spirit of despair" (Isaiah 61:3).

When you're hurting, be still and allow His healing love to permeate every fiber of your heart, even your whole being. As much as is possible, go about your daily tasks in the glad assurance of the loving presence of God, your adoring Father. He lavishes His love upon you and longs for you to know the certainty of His deep, eternal love for you, His precious child.

You may sometimes not feel God's loving favor,

You're Never Alone

but when He says He is *for* you and *with* you, He really means it.

Great is his love toward us, and the faithfulness of the LORD endures forever (Psalm 117:2).

When you feel most alone, the steadfast love of God will sustain you. Though your way seems rough and your days dark as night, His promises still hold. He assures you:

> I will lead the blind by ways they have not known, along unfamiliar paths I will guide them; I will turn the darkness into light before them and make the rough places smooth. These are the things I will do; I will not forsake them (Isaiah 42:16).

You are a child of the Most High. He created you to know His love. He invites you to rest in that love. More and more you will realize that your feelings are not indicators of reality. You never can be separated from God's eternal love. He loves you as much as He ever has loved the purest saint.

Absolutely nothing ever "will be able to separate us from the love of God that is in Christ Jesus our Lord" (Romans 8:39). You are His beloved. He will see you through. He holds the secret to a creative solution. Trust Him and wait expectantly.

When you pass through the waters, I will be with you; and when you pass through the rivers, they will not sweep over you. When you walk through the fire, you will not be burned (Isaiah 43:2).

*W*hile I was going through divorce and passing through the most difficult time of my life, I often felt that I would surely drown in my rivers of despair or be burned in the fire of adversity. God brought to my attention the above verse. I meditated on it day after day and found strength and encouragement.

I realized I had a choice of trying to work out my own situation and drowning in despair, or of trusting God's faithfulness. I chose to trust Him. He enabled me to swim through my dark waters until I reached the shore of safety. My problems did not work out as I had hoped, but God could see ahead and knew what was best for me.

Everyone goes through times of trouble and turmoil. That doesn't mean that God has forgotten us or that His power in our behalf is lessened. He loves us and will see us through the most difficult trials. His love and faithfulness never fail. We are never alone.

You're Never Alone

The LORD watches over you—the LORD is your shade at your right hand (Psalm 121:5).

*Y*our circumstances may cause you to wonder if God really does watch over you. God cannot lie. He is always true to Himself and to His Word. When unpleasant circumstances surround you, they look as if they will last forever. But they are like the morning fog that lifts when the sun comes out. The Lord is with you even in the midst of the fog.

You may feel as if you're in a dark prison that God will not enter. Never believe it. No place is too dark or too remote for the Lord to enter and rescue His own. Nor does it matter how long you have been there. He has been watching over you all the time. His love and His power are unlimited. His love for you is personal.

One day you will feel like the captives whom the Lord brought back to Zion. They said, "Our mouths were filled with laughter, our tongues with songs of joy.... The LORD has done great things for us, and we are filled with joy" (Psalm 126:2,3). That is the Lord's plan for you—to bring you back from captivity and fill you with His joy.

Therefore, I urge you, brothers, in view of God's mercy, to offer your bodies as living sacrifices, holy and pleasing to God—which is your spiritual worship (Romans 12:1).

*I*f you have gone through a divorce, you may feel unworthy to offer your body as a "living sacrifice" to God. But if you've repented of any part you might have had in your divorce, you are completely forgiven and cleansed—as if it had never happened. God desires your worship and praise of Him.

Such a crisis as divorce can strengthen your devotion to God, rather than weaken it, because you are in a position to realize your own utter helplessness and God's incredible faithfulness. Never cut yourself off from your church family, thinking they may criticize you. Those who know and love the Lord can support you as no one else can.

When you feel lonely, call a Christian friend who can lend a listening ear or offer encouragement. If you have no one you feel comfortable confiding in, ask the Lord to give you such a friend. In His time, He will lead you to such a one. Dare to see beyond your present limitations.

11

When Life Seems Futile

The eternal God is your refuge, and underneath are the everlasting arms (Deuteronomy 33:27).

*I*n despondency, Elizabeth Barrett Browning wrote:

> My heart is very tired—
> My strength is low—
> My hands are full of blossoms pluck'd
>   before
> Held dead within them till myself shall
>   die.

Do you sometimes feel as if you don't want to live another day? Everything seems so futile. You wonder, *What's the use? Why should I try anymore? I'm worn out. I've tried everything and nothing seems to be working.*

God wants to remind you that He is your refuge. He invites you to rest in His strong arms. He will give you the courage to go on. Keep reminding yourself that you are not alone. Understanding that and knowing God more intimately will help you to feel secure.

Refuse to focus on the suffering of the past. Live in God's love. Live in His Word. You can trust God and His sufficiency in every situation you face. You can make a fresh start, knowing that the everlasting arms of God are underneath you to support you. Ask the Lord to give you a new vision. Let Him plant a fresh purpose in your heart so that you may experience the new life He has promised.

You're Never Alone

"For I know the plans I have for you," declares the LORD, "plans to prosper you and not to harm you, plans to give you hope and a future" (Jeremiah 29:11).

*Y*ou feel as useless as a worn-out dishcloth. With your past being all it has been and all it should *not* have been, you wonder why you should even try to do or be anything worthwhile. When such thoughts come, remember God has a plan for your life—a plan to give you hope and a future. His plans are always good.

We all go through spiritual valleys. But we don't have to live there. God made us for higher planes. He is our encourager, ever present to urge us on. He never leaves us to climb out of the valleys alone. He provides the strength to go forward and upward.

Even though you have suffered years of disappointment, God is with you to help you rise above your feelings of futility. He has not forgotten you. The very things you have had to suffer have prepared you to be a more useful vessel in His service. Remind yourself often that God has a plan for your life. You can rest assured that His plans are always good, designed especially for you, His unique child.

Jesus came and stood among them and said, "Peace be with you!" (John 20:19).

Thomas, one of Jesus' disciples, felt especially deserted when Jesus was crucified and buried. He forgot that Jesus had told him and the other disciples that He would rise again. Even when the others told Thomas they had seen the risen Lord, he refused to believe them. His faith had been too badly shaken for him to risk being disappointed again. Life seemed utterly futile.

We can identify with Thomas. Many of us have had such painful experiences that we have difficulty believing. What happened to us has so shattered us that we are afraid to trust again. But just as Jesus appeared to Thomas and said not a word of condemnation, He comes to you and me and assures us of His loving presence. As He spoke peace to Thomas, so He speaks peace and assurance to our hearts.

Jesus is as close to us as He was to Thomas that day. Of course, Thomas saw Him in the flesh. We see Him with the eyes of faith. But He is no less real. He never leaves us alone or without His peace. He invites us to believe.

In all these things we are more than conquerors through him who loved us (Romans 8:37).

*P*aul mentioned a number of difficult things we might be faced with. Then he concluded by saying we are more than conquerors. In the process of recovery from any emotional hurt, we may be tempted to doubt that we can ever conquer our circumstances. Alone, we cannot. But with God's help, nothing is impossible.

God went ahead of His people when they left Egypt to enter into the promised land. He prepared the way for them. They could not see Him any more than we can. He made a way for them when there seemed to be no way. He will do the same for you and me. Every promise in the Bible is relevant to us because we belong to Him.

In our times of waiting for what seems impossible, God wants us to know He cares. His desire is to enfold us in His love, protect us by His power, and comfort us with His Spirit. His personal love for us is far greater than we can ever imagine. Unlike human love, God's love is always pure and holy. He not only desires the best for us, but He can also bring it about and make us more than conquerors.

How great is the love the Father has lavished on us, that we should be called children of God! And that is what we are! (1 John 3:1).

*I*f your past has been filled with disappointment and hurt, it is difficult to view yourself as the child of a loving God. It may seem more natural to see Him as a demanding tyrant than as a loving Father. You may tremble with fear in His presence, instead of knowing that He loves and accepts you as you are. Unless you know the heavenly Father's love, life seems futile.

God understands. He knows what happened to cause you to feel as you do. He doesn't say, "You shouldn't feel that way." He never condemns you for your feelings. God loves you as you are. He says, "My Son gave His life for you, and you are Mine. I have plans for your life."

If your life seems futile, be assured that God wants to give it meaning and purpose. God's loving-kindness never changes. He is ever and always a God of unconditional love. Regardless of what has happened and regardless of your feelings of futility, God wants to encourage you and give you meaningful goals.

In all your ways acknowledge him, and he will make your paths straight (Proverbs 3:6).

*W*hen life seems futile, we wonder which way to turn. God promises that when we acknowledge Him in all our ways, He will direct our paths. When we trusted Jesus as our personal Savior, He became the light of our life.

But feelings of futility come to the most faithful of God's children. Such feelings may cause us to take a negative view of ourselves. We sometimes suffer feelings of futility in reaction to adverse situations.

However, everything negative can change to positive. God wants us to remember that, as His beloved children, we are not alone. He cares. He bore not only our sins, but also our sorrows, even those regarding our negative feelings.

The prophet Isaiah says of the Lord, "You will keep in perfect peace him whose mind is steadfast, because he trusts in you" (Isaiah 26:3). Our Father wants to replace our feelings of futility with the awareness of His peace. Receiving His peace comes from learning to focus more and more on Him and His love and kindness.

You're Never Alone

"Continually restate to yourself what the purpose of your life is," says Oswald Chambers. Good counsel.

12

*When You're Tired
of Waiting*

But you, O Sovereign LORD, deal well with me for your name's sake; out of the goodness of your love, deliver me (Psalm 109:21).

*T*he Lord always deals well with His children, as the psalmist asked Him to do for him. Sometimes you wish you could see His hand at work. You find it especially difficult to wait when you're hurting on the inside. You wish you could speed up God's healing process. You want immediate deliverance. But as God is patient with you, He wants you to be patient with Him—for your good.

Our world encourages hurry and instant accomplishments. God does not fit into such a mold. He knows when to act quickly and when to work things out slowly. You can trust that He has a good reason for waiting. There may be a person related to your problem with whom He has to deal. Whatever the seeming delay, He knows what is best.

Because of His goodness and love, He *will* deliver you. Meanwhile, you may need to remind yourself often that He is with you. He has not forgotten you or your needs. He wants you to relax in His love and sense His reaching forth to take your cares.

Wait for the LORD; be strong and take heart and wait for the LORD (Psalm 27:14).

$\mathcal{M}$any years ago when I was in the hospital, a young man was brought into the room next to mine. Through the open door, I could hear him repeatedly crying out, "Why doesn't the doctor come? I need him *now*."

Whether we're hurting emotionally or physically, waiting is difficult. Yet, life is liberally punctuated with periods of waiting. That great man of prayer, Andrew Murray, said, "Be assured that if God waits longer than you could wish, it is only to make the blessing more precious."

The words sound praiseworthy. But it is not easy to trust in the Lord's ability to "make the blessing more precious" when we're waiting for Him to heal our hurts. We don't feel the depth of His care and understanding.

The Lord wants us to know He will not leave us even for a moment. He feels what we feel. His help will come in due time. His time schedule is perfect. While we wait, He surrounds us with His love. Our night will turn to day—in His perfect timing. In my life, those difficult times of waiting have always turned out for my best interest.

These [trials] have come so that your faith— of greater worth than gold, which perishes even though refined by fire—may be proved genuine and may result in praise, glory and honor when Jesus Christ is revealed (1 Peter 1:7).

*L*ast week I received a letter from a friend who has moved to a new location. She knew it wouldn't be easy to live there. It would bring back painful memories by placing her near to those who caused her hurts. But she sees God's hand in her move. She has grown stronger in faith through long periods of waiting for the Lord to act.

Some of us received the impression when we accepted salvation that becoming a Christian would automatically alleviate all pain and eliminate every trial. It doesn't, of course. We must wait for God to work in us. With His help, we *work through* our hurts as we grow in faith.

Life has times of difficulty for most of us. No one likes to wait for pain to end. But hurts produce fruit in our lives. The apostle Paul declares that suffering produces perseverance and leads to hope (Romans 5:3,4). When we are required to wait, we can be sure the Lord will provide strength for the waiting period.

He gives strength to the weary and increases the power of the weak (Isaiah 40:29).

*Y*ou read the above verse and wonder how long you'll have to wait for His strength to replace your weariness. You may feel that you've waited too long for His power to overcome your weakness. *Will it ever happen?* you ask yourself.

You want to recover from your problems today, not tomorrow or next year. You feel weary from waiting. You realize you didn't get the way you are overnight. But it's still a challenge to wait patiently for the healing process to work.

God intends that your waiting be a period of growing in your trust in Him. Waiting has rewards. Although it seems that nothing is happening, you can be assured that God is at work in your behalf. He will reward your quiet waiting.

The Lord promised through Isaiah that those who wait upon Him will renew their strength. His promises are true. Jeremiah said, "The LORD is good to those whose hope is in him, to the one who seeks him; it is good to wait quietly for the salvation of the LORD" (Lamentations 3:25,26).

Lead me in Your truth and teach me, for You are the God of my salvation; on You I wait all the day (Psalm 25:5 NKJV).

When I was struggling with inner pain several years ago, I often cried, "How long, oh God, how long must I wait?" No answer came. He wanted me to learn and grow through my dark waiting time. Our spiritual sight is sharper in the dark than in the light. The Lord is more interested in developing our spiritual sight than in hurrying our healing.

Most of us are called on to wait at one time or another. The psalmist knew the value of waiting. He declared that he waited on God all day. We know from Scripture that David waited *expectantly*. He knew that God would answer in His time. He also knew he was not alone. God was there.

Oswald Chambers said most of us know nothing about waiting. We simply endure. Those who wait patiently do so as David did—in the certainty of God's goodness.

Our waiting in the dark has a time limit known only to God. But we can be assured of His presence. He never leaves us alone in the dark. His love never fails.

You're Never Alone

How long, O LORD? Will you forget me forever? How long will you hide your face from me? (Psalm 13:1).

A new Christian went to a mature friend, complaining of her problems and the Lord's seeming slowness to answer. Her friend replied, "The Lord would not allow all these difficulties to come upon you if He didn't have confidence that you could handle them."

In frustration, the young woman answered, "Well, I wish the Lord didn't have such a high opinion of me."

Most of us have felt as that woman did or as the psalmist did when he cried, "How long will You forget me, Lord?"

In such times, we would do well to remember that feelings often have nothing to do with facts. The Scripture reminds us that God never so much as forgets a sparrow. How much more will He remember us!

As in David's life, our problems often seem greater than our ability to handle them. That's when we need to remind ourselves of Paul's words to the Romans that "we are more than conquerors through him who loved us" (Romans 8:37).

You're Never Alone

*I waited patiently for the LORD; he turned to
me and heard my cry* (Psalm 40:1).

The psalmist David probably knew as no other
Old Testament character (and certainly as none
of us ever has) what it meant to wait for the Lord to
act in his behalf. Again and again David cried to the
Lord for help, only to be required to wait.

It isn't that God turns a deaf ear to our cry. He
has reasons known only to Himself. We can be sure
it is always for our good.

Using the illustration of Abraham pitching his
tent toward Bethel and worshiping the Lord there,
Oswald Chambers says,

> We have to pitch our tents where we
> shall always have quiet times with God,
> however noisy our times with the world
> may be. There are not three stages in spir-
> itual life—worship, waiting and work....
> The three should go together.

Waiting goes with being a Christian living in a
fallen world. Our part is to trust God and do as
David did—wait patiently. Sooner or later we will

find that our patient waiting paid off for us, and often that it also benefited others.

13

When You Don't Know How to Pray

We do not know what to do, but our eyes are upon you (2 Chronicles 20:12 NIV).

When King Jehoshaphat heard that a vast army was coming against him, the king was alarmed. He proclaimed a fast and called the people together for prayer. He began his prayer by acknowledging the Lord's power and might. Then he prayed the above prayer.

Many times we don't know how or what to pray. King Jehoshaphat provides a good example for us. We are never to rush lightly into the Lord's presence. We first recognize that He is Lord of all and worthy of our praise. Then we are ready to make our request. Our prayer may be like Jehoshaphat's: "Lord, we do not know what to do, but our eyes are upon You."

The Lord honored the king's prayer of helplessness. He knows we're often weak and helpless when it comes to prayer. Just as Jehoshaphat must have prayed expecting God to answer, so can we. He will honor our prayer. In His love, He looks upon us and assures us that we're never alone in prayer. Even when we don't feel His presence, He is with us.

You're Never Alone

And surely I will be with you always, to the very end of the age (Matthew 28:20).

*I*f you feel that you don't know how to pray or if you have difficulty expressing your prayer in words, you may find encouragement in the writings of Leanne Payne, a widely recognized figure in the area of prayer ministry.

In her book *The Healing Presence*, Mrs. Payne says, "To acknowledge the Presence of *the God who is really there* is actually a form of prayer." She says that simply acknowledging the presence of God is a way of praying, which the Scriptures exhort us to do. In acknowledging God's presence, we are opening our eyes and ears to receive the word God is speaking to us. Prayer is dialogue.

Mrs. Payne goes on to explain that because of our intellectual blocks, "practicing the presence" requires discipline. Yet, practicing the presence of God is simply focusing on the truth that God is with us. What He said to the disciples right after His resurrection is true for us today. He is always with us—at prayer or whatever we're doing.

You're Never Alone

C.S. Lewis reminds us that it's the actual presence, not the sensation of the presence, "which begets Christ in us."

Then [Jesus] spoke a parable to them, that men always ought to pray and not lose heart (Luke 18:1 NKJV).

*A*re you sometimes concerned because you wonder if your prayers are long enough? Or beautiful enough? You need not be. It's the sincerity of your heart that counts. Let's forget about King James English when we pray. God wants us to simply be ourselves, expressing our prayers in whatever way is most natural for us.

The first moments of our day are most important. Our minds and bodies are usually fully rested at that time. Early morning is the time our minds are most receptive to whatever God might say to us.

Unless we begin our day in the awareness of God's presence, we are likely to do the very thing Jesus warned us against: "losing heart." Disciplining ourselves to quiet our minds and turn our thoughts to God the first thing in the morning is worth any effort it may take. Soon it will become a habit—a habit with which you'll never want to part. Turning our hearts to God upon waking helps us to keep in mind that He is always with us.

This is the assurance we have in approaching God: that if we ask anything according to his will, he hears us. And if we know that he hears us—whatever we ask—we know that we have what we asked of him (1 John 5:14,15).

"Sometimes I feel so alone when I pray," a friend said. "And too often nothing happens. Is my life so displeasing to God that He is angry with me and refuses to answer my prayers?"

"God is never angry with His people; He is only angry at sin," I replied. "God is a God of love and forgiveness, and He delights in responding lovingly to our prayers. Remember the psalmist's reminder: 'No good thing does he withhold from those whose walk is blameless' (Psalm 84:11). Sometimes His answer is delayed for one reason or another. But that is no reason for doubt."

James teaches us that we must ask in faith, and that our motives must be pure (James 1:6; 4:3). The Lord wants us always to ask *expectantly*, not doubting His presence or His desire to answer any prayer asked according to His will.

We are never alone when we come to God in prayer.

135

Enter his gates with thanksgiving and his courts with praise; give thanks to him and praise his name (Psalm 100:4).

A woman who was stunned by the sudden death of her husband quieted herself before the Lord and asked, "What do I do now?" In her broken heart, she seemed to hear God's strange reply: "Give thanks."

How could she? It wasn't easy. Finally, she knew she could thank God that her husband didn't have a lingering illness and that he was now at peace in the presence of God. She also thanked Him for the many years they had shared happily together.

Whatever our circumstances, we can find reasons to thank and praise God. I find that praising God for who He is and for all His goodness prepares my heart to pray more effectively. Praise helps us to focus on God and to be more receptive to His presence and His answers.

The psalmist said, "I will praise God's name in song and glorify him with thanksgiving" (Psalm 69:30). There's probably no better way to approach God in prayer than by thanking and praising Him in song.

May the righteous be glad and rejoice before God; may they be happy and joyful (Psalm 68:3).

*W*e can hardly read the book of Psalms without noticing that the psalmist David repeatedly refers to rejoicing in the Lord. He often began his prayers by expressing his joy to the Lord. It is evident that he *enjoyed* the Lord. Like all of us, David experienced times of depression when the Lord seemed far away, but he knew that in reality the Lord was always with him. His prayers indicate that he knew his joy was to be found in the Lord.

We cannot enjoy the Lord if we perceive Him as a harsh or punishing God. He is a loving Father who never leaves us alone. Some of us have attended church services where we often are reminded that our destiny is to enjoy God forever. If we are to enjoy God forever, isn't it reasonable to believe that we are to enjoy Him now—especially in our prayers?

Do not be anxious about anything, but in everything, by prayer and petition, with thanksgiving, present your requests to God (Philippians 4:6).

*D*o you worry about your weaknesses and become anxious over what you perceive as failures in prayer? If so, you're normal. The burden becomes heavier when you blame yourself. We sometimes expect more of ourselves than God does. When Paul told the Philippians not to worry about anything, he meant just that.

God's desire for His children is that we trust Him so completely that we stop worrying. That includes our distractions in prayer. If, while praying, your thoughts are interrupted by things you need to do, stop and make a note of them, then turn your thoughts back to God.

Good prayer promotes self-respect and produces a sweet spirit, says Reverend John Catoir. "All prayer is vain if it does not help you to love. To love, you must accept yourself, and to accept yourself, you must understand that you are an ordinary human being." Let's never be anxious over our lack of consistency in prayer. God understands. He is with us, never to leave us.

You're Never Alone

So Peter was kept in prison, but the church was earnestly praying to God for him (Acts 12:5).

*E*ven in the New Testament church, we sometimes see a lack of boldness in prayer. The church "was earnestly praying" for Peter. But we have no evidence that they were praying for his release from prison. Perhaps they only prayed for him to be sustained and strengthened. They, like us, sometimes neither knew *how* to pray or *what* to pray.

When an angel released Peter from prison, Peter went directly to the house where a group of Christians had gathered to pray for him. He knocked on the door. When the servant girl went to answer, she returned and told the group that Peter was at the door.

" 'You're out of your mind,' they told her. When she kept insisting that it was so, they said, 'It must be his angel' " (Acts 12:15).

How many times do we pray without expecting the Lord to answer, even beyond our hopes? We forget that He "is able to do immeasurably more than all we ask or imagine, according to his power that is at work within us" (Ephesians 3:20).

You're Never Alone

In this manner, therefore, pray... (Matthew 6:9 NKJV).

*J*esus followed His above words with what is known as the model prayer. I would like to suggest that if He were speaking audibly to you and me today, He might add, "Pray in the way that is natural and right for you individually."

I've had to learn the hard way to be myself without copying somebody else's ideas—even in prayer. Someone said, "Pray as you can, not as you can't." When we pray the way someone else suggests, we may be praying "as we can't." That is, we may be simply parroting words without actually praying. We need to let go of perceived notions of prayer and come before God as little children.

In her book, *Pray As You Can,* Jean Gill says,

> God is infinite and can enter into our lives
> in an infinite variety of ways. When we
> restrict the ways we pray, we restrict the
> ways we will allow God to touch us....
> We have much in common with others,
> and so we can all use some basic ways of
> prayer.... But we need to adapt these
> ways to our own individuality. Each of us

is a unique and special person, and we
need to find our own ways of prayer.

14

*When Your
Bible Reading
Seems Empty*

Do not let this Book of the Law depart from your mouth; meditate on it day and night, so that you may be careful to do everything written in it (Joshua 1:8).

*H*ow can I meditate on something that has so little meaning to me? I read through the Bible once, but came out no better for it," a friend confided. "So I've given up trying to read it anymore."

The Bible can mean only as much to us as we determine to make it a priority. If we read the Bible or any portion of it only to say we've read it, our reading can profit little. We must have a desire to know the One who inspired the writings of the Book before it can speak meaningfully to us.

God's Word is more than a collection of long-ago happenings. God wants to speak personally to us through His written Word. "For the word of God is living and active. Sharper than any double-edged sword, it penetrates even to dividing soul and spirit, joints and marrow; it judges the thoughts and attitudes of the heart" (Hebrews 4:12).

When we read our Bible expectantly, God can speak to our hearts through its pages.

You're Never Alone

He who has ears to hear, let him hear! (Matthew 13:9 NKJV).

God has given to everyone spiritual ears. The choice is ours as to how and whether we use them to hear Him. He especially speaks through His written Word. Unless our ears are open and our concentration focused, our reading of the Word may seem empty.

Part of concentration means getting rid of anything that may distract our minds. Radio, television, and telephone can be real hindrances. A friend confided that he finds himself turning on the TV in the middle of his Bible reading and prayer time. Of course his thoughts are interrupted, and he decides to give up and go to work.

The spiritual enemy of our souls works overtime to keep us from reading and hearing the Word of God. Our alertness to his tactics can be of help when it comes time for our daily Bible reading time.

Regardless of any obstacles, let's never give up our practice of Bible reading and study. God is never nearer to us than when we're reading His Word and listening for His voice.

You're Never Alone

Trust in the LORD with all your heart and lean not on your own understanding (Proverbs 3:5).

*T*he only way we can trust in the Lord with all our hearts and avoid leaning on our own understanding is to trust His wisdom as we read His Word. The Bible is full of gems of truth. We have only to search them out and let them become light for us.

A working mother told me, "I have little time to read my Bible. I just read it a few minutes every morning wherever it happens to fall open."

I can understand her challenge. I, too, used to be a working mother. I found that the only way I could have a meaningful Bible reading time was to rise a few minutes earlier than usual and deliberately read a passage until I saw something that applied to me. Then I'd spend a brief time meditating on that particular thought. That gave me strength for the day.

The Bible is a book about God and His love and about people with problems like ours. For all who take time to read it meditatively, it is a treasure house of truth, hope, peace, and direction.

Let the word of Christ dwell in you richly in all wisdom (Colossians 3:16 NKJV).

W hen we approach the Word of God, we are to *expect* it to do what God intended—take root in us and become living bread to feed our souls. Only then can it dwell in our hearts "richly in all wisdom."

Opening my Bible each morning, I often ask the Holy Spirit to show me what He wants to show me in my reading for the day.

Many of us sang in childhood,

> Read your Bible every day,
> Praying as you read it.
> It will guide you on your way,
> If you'll only heed it.

There's much more truth in those words than any of us realized when we sang the chorus in childhood. It takes an open heart and an open mind to hear what God is saying to us in His Word. He delights to show us His truth and to cause His words to dwell in our hearts at all times.

When the psalmist said the Word was a light to his path, he wasn't parroting empty words. The

Holy Spirit can give us fresh insight if we ask Him to, as we read the Word which He inspired.

You're Never Alone

I wait for the L̲O̲R̲D̲, my soul waits, and in his word I put my hope (Psalm 130:5).

*T*he psalmists were as human as you and I. Yet the writer of this psalm knew where to put his hope. When we come to the Word of God with hope in our hearts, we will not be disappointed.

The Bible, of course, is different from any other book ever written. In it we can indeed put our hope. We need to be aware of that truth every time we come to read our Bibles. The Bible shows us over and over the mercy of God. He always dealt mercifully with His people. He shows the same mercy to us who have put our trust in Him for our salvation.

The Bible assures us again and again that God is our loving Father, wanting always to reveal His unconditional love to us. He reveals His love by His Spirit and through His written Word.

Reading the Bible for personal devotions and making our time with Him our number-one priority pays off. "He is a rewarder of those who diligently seek Him" (Hebrews 11:6 NKJV). We can depend on that truth.

You're Never Alone

The entrance of your words gives light; it gives understanding to the simple (Psalm 119:130).

When your Bible reading seems empty, you might like to try what many other people have found successful: Let the Scriptures you read become your personal prayers. Of course, not all Scriptures lend themselves to such practice, but you can find many that do—especially in Paul's writings and in the book of Psalms.

You might start by looking at some of Paul's prayers and making them your own. For example, he told the Ephesians that he prayed that God would strengthen them and reveal the depth of His love for them (see Ephesians 3:16-19). I often re-word that prayer to say:

> I pray that out of His glorious riches He may strengthen me with power through His Spirit in my inner being, so that Christ may dwell in my heart through faith. And that I, being rooted and established in love, may have power...to grasp how wide and long and high and deep is the love of Christ, and to know this love that surpasses knowledge.

Paul begins most of his letters with "Grace and peace to you." You and I can accept that as God's desire for us.

*Sing joyfully to the L*O*RD, you righteous; it is*
fitting for the upright to praise him (Psalm 33:1).

*H*ave you ever considered using your Bible as
a hymnal or as a means of praising the Lord?
The book of Psalms is sometimes referred to as the
book of praise. Many of the psalms are expressions
of praise to God for who He is and for what He has
done.

You may think, "God doesn't need praise from
little old me." But God never feels that you're small
or insignificant. You are special to Him, and He delights to hear you praise Him. What better way to
do that than through the use of Scripture?

Reading the book of Psalms, you'll notice how
often the psalmists praise the Lord. David said, "I will
extol the LORD at all times; his praise will always be
on my lips" (Psalm 34:1). Throughout that psalm,
he mentioned things for which he praised the Lord.

In the familiar Psalm 139, David said, "I praise
you because I am fearfully and wonderfully made. . . .
All the days ordained for me were written in your
book before one of them came to be" (Psalm 139:14,
16). As we recall all that the Lord has done for us,

even before our birth, doesn't it summon forth our praise and adoration?

When anyone hears the message [of the Word of God] and does not understand it, the evil one comes and snatches away what was sown in his heart (Matthew 13:19).

If we are passive in our spiritual outlook, we are likely to retain very little of what we read. We can begin by asking the Lord to prepare our hearts and make us sensitive to His voice as we read.

One way we can enrich our understanding and quicken our interest in the Bible is to read from several translations. I use about 15 different translations.

It's fun to compare the various versions. For example, Romans 12:2 is a passage you might like to compare and notice the slight differences: "Do not conform any longer to the pattern of this world, but be transformed by the renewing of your mind." "Don't let the world around you squeeze you into its own mold, but let God remold you from within" (PHILLIPS). "Do not model yourselves on the behavior of the world around you, but let your behavior change, remodeled by your new mind" (JERUSALEM BIBLE). "Adapt yourselves no longer to the pattern of this present world, but let your minds be remade and your whole nature thus transformed" (NEB).

15

When You Feel
Worthless

For he chose us in him before the creation of the world. . . . In love he predestined us to be adopted as his sons (Ephesians 1:4).

I'm so worthless," a Christian friend said to me. "I don't feel that I'm of any value to God or anyone else."

"You believe the Bible, don't you?" I asked.

"Certainly," she said. "You know I do."

"Haven't you noticed that God values you?"

She had never seen that fact.

Most of us have had times when we felt valueless. We think we're too insignificant, too inadequate, too inferior, too one thing or another. Would God, who knows all things, have chosen us before the creation of the world and adopted us to be His very own if He had thought we would ever be valueless?

The very fact that we are created in God's image makes us valuable. That Jesus willingly shed His blood for us further reveals the value He places on us. Regardless of our feelings, we are God's priceless creation.

He places so much value on us that He never leaves us alone.

Before I formed you in the womb I knew you, before you were born I set you apart (Jeremiah 1:5).

"How do you know you're loved and valuable?" a young would-be evangelist asked a stranger.

"Because I'm here," came the immediate answer. That's right. You wouldn't be here if you were not loved and valuable to God. God chose to create you to be His beloved child. Nothing can keep you from being valuable to Him.

The words spoken to Jeremiah in the above Scripture apply to you and me. We are so valuable to God that even before we were conceived in the womb, He set us apart for Himself.

Valuing yourself as a member of God's family is not an attitude of superiority. Biblical self-love recognizes that on your own you are helpless and worthless, but at the same time recognizes that through Christ you are strong and worthy.

We need never judge ourselves by our own weak feelings about ourselves. Let us learn to view ourselves through the eyes of our loving Father. We can rejoice in knowing He has adopted us as His very own.

160

You're Never Alone

Who knows whether you have come to the king-dom for such a time as this? (Esther 4:14 NKJV).

*G*od called Queen Esther to save her people from extermination by the Persians. When Esther's stepfather, Mordecai, realized what was about to happen to the Jews, he sent word to Esther asking her to use her influence to save herself and her people.

As surely as God had a purpose for Esther and for each man and woman of the Bible, He has a purpose for you. You are valuable to Him and in His service. You might do well to ask yourself the question that Mordecai asked Esther: "Who knows whether you are here for such a time as this?"

Whatever the reason for your coming into the world, God ordained your birth for a purpose. You are much more valuable to Him than you can ever imagine.

"Our attitude toward ourselves—our self-concept or our self-image—is one of the most important things we possess," says Christian psychologist Bruce Larson. Mr. Larson explains that misguided people have drilled into us that it's wrong for us to have a positive attitude about ourselves. God does. So why shouldn't we?

You're Never Alone

You are not alone, even though you may feel worthless.

I am not conscious of anything against my-self, and I feel blameless (1 Corinthians 4:4 AMP).

*D*oes that sound as if Paul was boasting? He wasn't. Paul simply knew his value in Christ. He accepted himself without putting himself down, as you and I are prone to do. Why should we not feel as Paul did, when we know we have Christ living within and that we are living for Him?

Threats to our peace of mind regarding our self-worth come from our distorted understanding. Author Vincent Collins defines such a threat as "an unsuspected, sabotaging fifth columnist who is right inside you." He says this fifth columnist is the feelings with which we must deal. Such feelings are the reason for our self-doubt. We need to remember that feelings are not always fact.

Self-reproachful feelings argue with the Word of God. When my feelings tell me something about myself that does not line up with what the Bible says, it's time for me to be still and know that God is God, and meditate on who I am in Christ. A thorough grasp of God's love and appreciation for us can transform our image of ourselves. Such an understanding can help us to realize that we are never alone because we know that God is always with us.

Be transformed by the renewing of your mind (Romans 12:2 NKJV).

We may transform our view of ourselves and come to a better understanding of how valuable we are to God by reading His Word, meditating on it, and noticing how He indicates over and over that He loves and cares for us. When Jesus walked here on earth, He demonstrated His love for God's children every day. He has not changed.

Some people get the idea from reading the Old Testament that God is a wrathful God. But God's wrath is never poured out on His beloved children, but only upon those who deliberately rebel against Him. God constantly seeks to reveal His love to us. He wants us to know that He values us and that we can value ourselves without feeling guilty.

Minister and Christian author Bruce Larson believes that the solution to many of our personal problems lies in a better attitude toward ourselves. He says, "If we can only like ourselves, then our discouragements, hostilities and anxieties will begin to fade." Let's get a better grasp of God's love and be transformed.

You're Never Alone

You are someone special, especially to God. Dare to believe it. It's true.

You're Never Alone

I have loved you with an everlasting love; I have drawn you with loving-kindness (Jeremiah 31:3).

"Choose me! Choose me!" clamored my third-graders as the team captains chose sides for the class spelling match. A little later, on the playground getting ready to play softball, they again cried, "Choose me." To my dismay, the less gifted were almost always the last to be chosen.

Bobby was among the poor spellers. But it never seemed to bother him that he usually was chosen last in the spelling matches. Maybe it was because he knew he was an excellent ball player, and he didn't need to excel in everything. Bobby was an encourager. When a teammate struck out, Bobby would put his arm around him and say, "That's okay. You'll do better next time."

That's what Jesus does for you and me. When we accept the Lord's invitation to play on His team, He encourages us. He says, "I love you with an everlasting love. I have chosen you with lovingkindness."

When we see ourselves as worthless, we are likely to struggle with self-acceptance. Let's acknowledge our strengths and our weaknesses, knowing that God never sees us as worthless, but as His beloved.

You're Never Alone

*What is man that you are mindful of him? . . .
You made him a little lower than the heavenly
beings and crowned him with glory and honor*
(Psalm 8:4,5).

When I heard three ministers in different settings refer to the above verses, I took another look at those words. Think about it! God has made us a little lower than the angels and crowned us with glory and honor. What a boost that should give to our self-esteem! What value God places on us!

Those verses can remind us again that we are created in the image of God, that He is Spirit and has given us a spirit because He wants to commune with us. We are the only creatures that have the privilege of hearing God and communing with Him who created the universe.

The Lord's acceptance of us is a free gift of His love. We are made worthy through His Son, Jesus. Through the written Word and by His Spirit, He tells us again and again that we are valuable. Since our Father sees us as valuable, let's ignore the negative suggestions of our minds and agree with what our heavenly Father says about us.

Therefore, if anyone is in Christ, he is a new creation.... God made him who had no sin to be sin for us, so that in him we might become the righteousness of God (2 Corinthians 5:17, 21).

We have a spiritual enemy who never tires of tempting us to doubt our worth. Since he knows he can't get to Christ, he works overtime to get to His chosen ones to make us doubt our worth. He even tries to blind our eyes to what the Savior has done for us through the cross.

It's up to us to continually remind ourselves of what God says about us. Because of God's love for us, He has made us new creatures in Christ. He inspired Paul to write that we are the very righteousness of God. It sounds incredible, doesn't it? But it's true.

God never compares us with anybody else. When I get to heaven, God will not say to me, "Marie, why were you not like Lydia or Dorcas?" Having been justified by the blood of Jesus, I don't expect to be asked any *whys*. But it wouldn't be unreasonable to be asked, "Why didn't you value yourself?"

People cannot supply our feelings of self-worth, but God can.

For as high as the heavens are above the earth, so great is his love for those who fear him (Psalm 103:11).

*I*f anyone ever had reason to feel worthless, it must have been Gomer, the unfaithful wife of Hosea (see the book of Hosea in the Old Testament). In the eyes of everyone except her husband, she was a worthless nobody. God used Hosea's love for his repeatedly erring wife to show the depth of His divine love for His people. Even if others see us as worthless, God sees possibilities in us.

When human love would give up, God's love continues steadfast. We tend to compare God's value of us with our own, but God's love and the value He places on us is far beyond comparison.

"For as high as the heavens are above the earth, so great is his love for those who fear him. . . . From everlasting to everlasting the LORD's love is with those who fear him" (Psalm 103:11,17).

Our worth comes from the One who loved us enough to give Himself for us. God looks at us through the shed blood of His Son. Nothing can change the way He sees us. But our attitude toward ourselves affects the quality of our relationship with our loving heavenly Father.

When they measure themselves by themselves and compare themselves with themselves, they are not wise (2 Corinthians 10:12).

We need to feel good about ourselves in order to live joyously as God intended. Poor self-esteem causes us to compare ourselves unfavorably with other people, as Scripture advises us against. When we compare ourselves with another, we usually measure our weak points against his or her strong ones.

I have a friend who loves me and accepts me just as I am—weaknesses and all. When I am with her, I am free to be myself. I don't need to wear a facade, so I enjoy being with her.

The same should be true in our relationship with God. When we know that He values us and accepts us just as we are, we enjoy fellowship with Him. Studies show that those persons with a high level of self-esteem view God as loving and kind. A healthy self-image helps us to relate more maturely to God and to other people. We can stop feeling as if we have to compete or earn acceptance. More importantly, a proper evaluation of ourselves frees us to fulfill the purposes God has for us.

You're Never Alone

The kingdom of God is within you (Luke 17:21).

*I*f we could fully grasp the meaning of Jesus' words that the kingdom of God is within us, it would change our view of ourselves. We would stop feeling that we are of no value.

Some humanists say that if we have felt put-down all our lives, especially in childhood, we are locked into having to cope and adjust in the best way we can. But the Lord offers a way out. That doesn't mean we won't have a period of working through our past. But we won't have to do it alone. God is with us to help us. He will lead us. We can come to an understanding of who we are in Him.

Meanwhile, we can give ourselves permission to be ourselves, joyously. We can start valuing our own opinions without having to consult someone else before we make every decision, large or small.

Meditating on God's personal love for us enables us to think more highly of ourselves. The more securely we are grounded in God's love and in the knowledge of our identity with Him, the more we are able to accept and value ourselves as God does.

173

16

When You Can't Hear God Speak

The Lord came and stood there, calling...
"Samuel! Samuel!" then Samuel said, "Speak,
for your servant is listening" (1 Samuel 3:10).

*S*amuel was only a child the first time he heard the Lord speak. His mother had taken him to the temple where he "ministered before the Lord under Eli." The first two times Samuel heard the Lord, he thought it was the voice of Eli the priest. Eli explained that the voice was the Lord's. When the boy heard the voice the third time, he answered as Eli had told him: "Speak, for your servant is listening."

One of the most precious privileges we have as Christians is to hear God speak. However, we sometimes mistake other voices for the voice of the Lord, as the child Samuel did. How can we distinguish the voice of the Lord from other voices, or from our own thoughts?

The Lord's voice to His faithful followers is always gentle, loving, and full of compassion. His voice is always consistent with His written Word. Sometimes we fail to hear the Lord's voice because we are not *still* enough. His voice is almost always very quiet. He does speak to His children.

Be still, and know that I am God (Psalm 46:10).

There's much more in the above verse than we may see at first. God reveals Himself to those who learn to achieve inner and outer quiet. He speaks to those who quietly and expectantly listen for His voice. But as Dr. Charles Stanley says, "If we are not listening, we won't hear a sound."

I referred in an earlier chapter to a friend who became so frustrated with life that she prayed for God to stop the world and let her off. Perhaps many of us have felt that way but have not dared to voice it. God may be saying to us in such times, "Be still, and know that I am God."

Another friend told me she was "too busy" for a daily quiet time until she had a heart attack. Now she's grateful for that illness because it led her to a deeper walk with the Lord. She's learning to be still, rest in the Lord, and listen to His voice. She knows the Lord did not cause her illness. She brought it on herself by her busyness. But the Lord used it to teach her how to hear His voice.

Let's listen daily for that tremendously quiet voice. We'll be glad we did.

Listen carefully to the voice of the LORD your God and do what is right in his eyes (Exodus 15:26).

*F*rom the beginning of time, God has spoken to His people. In this day it seems more difficult for us to hear God's voice than in Bible times. Perhaps in those days God's people made a habit of listening more carefully than we do today. If we are to hear God speak, we must cultivate a habit of listening for His voice.

God wants us to listen to Him, confident of His love, not fearful and trying to hide from Him as Adam and Eve did in the Garden of Eden after they had disobeyed Him. When we hear and obey God's voice, we have no reason to be afraid. If we disobey, all He asks is that we repent and receive His forgiveness and the restoration of our joy.

God speaks in various ways: through His written Word, through His anointed servants, and through direct revelation in our inner being. Paul prayed for the Ephesians, asking God to give them the Spirit of wisdom and revelation, so that they might know

Him better (Ephesians 1:17). Obviously, we will
know Him better as we learn to listen to His voice.

My soul, wait silently for God alone, for my expectation is from Him" (Psalm 62:5 NKJV).

Many times in Scripture we are told to wait for God. The psalmist spoke to his soul, telling it to wait silently for God. God seldom (if ever) gets in a hurry. In our impatience, we often hurry, which leads to trouble.

We don't wait for the still, quiet voice of God before acting. This is more often true of new Christians than for those who are mature. But any of us can develop an ear for hearing God speak and learn to distinguish His voice from another's.

The voice of our spiritual enemy, Satan, urges us to make decisions quickly without waiting for God's direction. Anytime that we feel an overwhelming urge to act quickly, we probably would do well to wait. The voice of the enemy may be tempting us.

We can always be sure that whatever we hear from God is what is best for us. God's voice usually produces a tranquil spirit within us. When we wait for Him and follow His instructions, He gives a peace that passes understanding.

You're Never Alone

God invites us to come to Him as a trusting child to his or her father and listen for His quiet voice.

The fear of the LORD is the beginning of wisdom; a good understanding have all those who do His commandments (Psalm 111:10 NKJV).

To fear the Lord is to have a deep reverence for Him. If we are to hear the Lord speak, we must reverence Him, stand in awe of Him, knowing that He is worthy of our listening. There is none like Him. As we listen in sincerity for the Lord's voice, we acknowledge that we are creatures of the most high God, and that He desires to speak to His children and give us direction in life.

When our minds and hearts are open to the majesty of God, we realize that we stand before not only a holy God, but also One who is willing and desirous of speaking to us. He is pleased when we come before Him expecting to hear Him speak.

17

When Your Joy Has Gone

In Your presence is fullness of joy; at Your right hand are pleasures forevermore (Psalm 16:11 NKJV).

*D*o you sometimes read Scriptures such as the above and feel that they do not apply to you? Most of us have times like that. Sometimes the news we hear is enough to take away our joy. A friend says she never listens to the news on TV; it fills her with such despair. I admit I often feel that way, too. However, when we hear of evil going on in the world, we can know that Scripture is being fulfilled.

The secret of finding joy in the midst of turmoil is to fix our eyes on the Lord and realize that He is with us. In His presence "is fullness of joy." Our Father does not want us to walk around with the weight of the world on our shoulders.

When I'm told to fix my eyes on the Lord, I sometimes think of Paul's words to the Philippians: "Whatever is pure, whatever is lovely, whatever is admirable—if anything is excellent or praiseworthy— think about such things" (Philippians 4:8).

You're Never Alone

I have to discipline my mind to think on what is lovely, admirable, and praiseworthy. When I do, my joy is restored.

*I have told you this so that my joy may be in you
and that your joy may be complete* (John 15:11).

Near the equator between the areas of the north-east and southeast trade winds over the ocean lies a region of air called the "doldrums," meaning "dullness." Sailing vessels of the early days were often stranded there for weeks without a breeze to fill their sails.

Many of us sometimes get caught in spiritual doldrums. Life becomes dull and all joy disappears. We wish for a joyful breeze to fill our spiritual sails, but we find none. We live in a world where uncertainty abounds. That's one reason we have to guard against sailing into the doldrums.

Unlike the old sailing vessels, we are not helpless. We can recall Jesus' words to His disciples and know that He has told us things to make our joy complete. Jesus warned that we would experience times of discouragement. He Himself became discouraged, but He never allowed Himself to slip into the doldrums. He knew that God was in control. We, too, can rest in the harbor of God's love until the sailing is clear and we're back to smooth gliding.

*Sing to the L*ORD*, you saints of his; praise his holy name. . . . Rejoicing comes in the morning* (Psalm 30:4,5).

*I*t's going to be joyous year," a young woman said as she hung a new calendar on the wall.

"How do you know?" her visiting friend asked.

"I know it is because I'm going to take one day at a time and make it joyous. I'm going to begin every morning by praising the Lord and thanking Him for a new day."

We know that our days will be anything but joyful if we try to live our tomorrows today, as many of us are prone to do. Jeremiah said of the Lord, "His compassions never fail. . . . They are new every morning; great is your faithfulness" (Lamentations 3:22,23).

Whatever each day holds, we can be sure of the Lord's compassions and His faithfulness. His love is steadfast. He is always with us. If we allow our feelings to rule us, joy may elude us. We cannot afford to be guided by our feelings if we are to live joyfully. We must take charge and *decide* to live joyfully, in spite of our feelings or circumstances. My life can become burdensome if I take my eyes off

Jesus. When I remember that God is present with
His love and joy, life takes on a new perspective.

*Shout aloud and sing for joy, people of Zion,
for great is the Holy One of Israel among you*
(Isaiah 12:6).

Some of us have greater difficulty than others in remembering to sing for joy, keeping in mind the greatness of the Lord. When things are not going our way, we forget the greatness of the Holy One. We would rather do anything than sing.

Two brothers spoke at a retreat I attended. One always radiated optimism. Joy shone on his face and flowed from his lips. His brother, on the other hand, told us he had a built-in radar for picking up negative messages. He said, "If ten people tell me they enjoyed my talk, and one tells me he didn't get a thing out of it, I forget the nine and remember the one negative comment."

At the end of your day, what events do you recall most vividly—the positive or the negative? If you answered, "The negative," you might like to practice what other people have successfully tried. Before falling asleep at night, take a few minutes to reflect on your day. Recall when you felt the Lord's love and presence most distinctly. Relive

that moment and thank God for it. Then ask the
Lord to show you how you can benefit from the
not-so-beautiful events.

Burst into songs of joy together, you ruins of Jerusalem, for the LORD has comforted his people, he has redeemed Jerusalem (Isaiah 52:9).

Although the above verse was addressed to Jerusalem, it may well apply to you and me individually. There are times when we feel that our life is in ruins. But the word of the Lord to us is, "Burst into songs of joy." Why? How can we? Because the Lord is present to comfort us and restore our joy, just as He was for Jerusalem. Without Him, there is no reason for real joy.

Oswald Chambers said,

> The full flood of my life is not in bodily health, not in external happenings, not in seeing God's work succeed, but in the perfect understanding of God, and in the communion with Him that Jesus Himself had.... Be rightly related to God, find your joy there, and out of you will flow rivers of living water.

We cannot control what happens to us, but we can control our response to what happens. The power of the Lord is with us because He has redeemed us and enabled us to "burst into songs of joy." He dwells eternally within us to fill us with the kind of joy that He alone can give. Let us accept it.

The joy of the LORD is your strength (Nehemiah 8:10).

*A*fter the walls of Jerusalem had been rebuilt following the city's destruction, the people gathered to hear Ezra the priest read the law of Moses. When the people realized the extent of their sins against God and His wonderful mercies to them, they repented, mourned, and wept.

Seeing their repentance, the governor, Nehemiah, said, "This day is sacred to our Lord. Do not grieve, for the joy of the LORD is your strength." Then he told them it was time to celebrate.

There is a time for mourning over mistakes and failures, but the Lord does not want His children to continue groveling in misery. His desire for us is joy. It is fitting for us to celebrate His goodness when we understand what He has done for us.

He says He will "provide for those who grieve in Zion—to bestow on them a crown of beauty instead of ashes, the oil of gladness instead of mourning, and a garment of praise instead of a spirit of despair" (Isaiah 61:3).

You're Never Alone

The psalmist said, "In Your presence is fullness of joy; at Your right hand are pleasures forevermore" (Psalm 16:11 NKJV).

. . . so that I may finish my race with joy, and the ministry which I received from the Lord Jesus (Acts 20:24 NKJV).

The apostle Paul knew he had been given a ministry. His one desire was to be sure he had finished what he had been given to do before his departure from this earth. I am especially impressed with his words "that I may finish my race *with joy."*

Each of us was created do something that we enjoy doing. The Lord has given each of us a ministry, something that only *we* can accomplish in His kingdom. We feel unfulfilled until we're doing what the Lord created us to do.

At times we allow our negative thoughts about ourselves to rob us of joy. We have the option of cooperating with our higher self—the joyous person God created us to be—or of cooperating with our spiritual enemy and becoming our own enemy by depriving ourselves of the joy of the Lord. Positive, God-inspired thoughts help promote inner joy.

My servants will sing out of the joy of their hearts (Isaiah 65:14).

*T*he great musician Joseph Haydn was asked why his church music was so cheerful. He replied, "When I think upon God, my heart is so full of joy that the notes dance and leap from my pen."

A heart that has been healed of its subconscious wounds may dance for joy like the notes of Haydn's music. But too often our past has so distorted the face of God that our hearts are unable to dance when we think of Him.

Many years ago I sat in a church service and listened to the music director as he exhorted us to "smile as you sing." I'm sure I wasn't the only person who thought, "Wouldn't it be hypocritical for me to paste a smile on my face when there's no smile inside?"

When the joy of the Lord fills our souls, our faces light up when we think of Him. It's when we are assured of our Father's unconditional love that we can find real joy.

Oswald Chambers said that Jesus does not come to us and say, "Cheer up." He plants within us "the miracle of joy of God's own nature. The miracle of the Christian life is that God can give man joy in the midst of external misery."

18

*When Illness
Lingers*

Be still before the LORD and wait patiently for him (Psalm 37:7).

*N*ot long ago I had to remind myself often to wait patiently for the Lord. A physical problem struck me and lingered on. When you know that something is wrong with your body, it isn't easy to wait patiently. The doctors were doing all they could, but my body responded slowly.

No one chooses to endure a lingering illness. Yet, it unexpectedly happens to many of us. At such times we can rely only on the grace and encouragement that comes from God. John tells us, "From the fullness of his grace we have all received one blessing after another" (John 1:16). During my lengthy recovery period, I had to lean heavily on God's promise of grace and blessing.

I have found that in trying times when physical problems refuse to go away, I can become more aware of God's abundant grace and His promise to be with me. I reminded myself often of His promise in Hebrews 13:5. I meditated especially on the Amplified translation: "I will not in any way fail you nor give you up nor leave you without support. [I

will] not, [I will] not, [I will] not in any degree leave
you helpless nor forsake nor let [you] down."

Whoever listens to me will live in safety and be at ease, without fear of harm (Proverbs 1:33).

*D*uring my lengthy recovery period from illness, I sometimes became fearful. It seemed that my problem would never go away. I silently quoted the above verse over and over. But I *was* afraid "of harm"—afraid I would never be completely over my physical ailment. In the midst of my lingering illness, I was sometimes tempted to doubt that the promises of God applied to my particular situation. Yet I knew the promises were true because God is faithful and never breaks one of His promises.

For several days after I went home from the hospital, I didn't even feel like picking up my Bible. I was thankful for the Word I had hidden in my heart. Many years previously I had memorized the 16 verses of Psalm 91. I can no longer quote the entire psalm, but certain promises stood out clearly in my mind and encouraged me:

> He who dwells in the secret place of the
> Most High shall abide under the shadow
> of the Almighty.... No evil shall befall

you. . . . For He shall give His angels
charge over you. . . . He shall call upon
Me, and I will answer him; I will be with
him in trouble (Psalm 91:1,10,11,15 NKJV).

I am the LORD, your God, who takes hold of your right hand and says to you, Do not fear; I will help you (Isaiah 41:13).

Again and again during my recovery period, I experienced setbacks. That's when the above verse became especially meaningful to me. Our human tendency when we recognize that our bodies are functioning abnormally is to focus on our problem. I became fearful, even though I knew there was nothing I could do about my situation.

One day the Lord brought to my mind the words of Proverbs 17:22: "A happy heart is good medicine and a cheerful mind works healing" (AMP). It's hard to have a happy heart or a cheerful mind when your body is healing more slowly than you or your doctor expected it to. The only way I could do that was to stop focusing on my problem and realize that God was holding my hand, caring for me.

I recalled Romans 8:31: "If God is for us, who can be against us?" I reworded the verse to say, "If God is for me, *what* can be against me?" God is more powerful than anything that can touch us in spirit, soul, or body. I agree with whoever said that

You're Never Alone

we are bound to encounter troubles, but we don't have to be broken by them.

We are hard pressed on every side, but not crushed; perplexed, but not in despair; persecuted, but not abandoned; struck down, but not destroyed (2 Corinthians 4:8,9).

Sometimes when we experience a lingering illness, we feel perplexed and in despair. Paul said he was perplexed but *not* in despair. Most of us have not grown to such an extent that our perplexities don't cast us into despair.

Several years ago I received a letter from an unknown woman with a desperate cry. She felt that her world had crumbled and fallen apart. She saw no way out of her despair. I prayed for her, and we continued corresponding. Little by little her letters were bathed in fewer tears.

One day I received her letter written on cheery yellow stationery. She began, "Each day brings a new way to praise the Lord! I have found peace. Thank you for your prayers while I was putting my life back together."

Her circumstances had not changed, but she had. God is in the business of putting lives back together even in the midst of pain and suffering.

Jesus voluntarily went through suffering—both physical and emotional—so that we might experience victory in spite of present trials.

But seek first the kingdom of God and His righteousness, and all these things shall be added to you (Matthew 6:33 NKJV).

*W*hen we're hurting and wanting more than anything to recover from a lingering illness, it isn't easy to seek first the kingdom of God. How can we? Only by remembering that God is with us and that He cares. He is concerned about everything that concerns us. While our bodies may be wracked by pain, it is possible for our spirits to rise above our bodily feelings.

A few years ago I kept in touch with a friend whose problems seemed unending. As soon as one problem cleared up, another arose. One day I received a letter containing a typical message: "Things have gone from bad to worse. But in spite of the pressures, God has been with me and upheld me."

A short time later another letter came from my friend:

> The events that occur daily have not changed, but my attitude has. Above all else, I have experienced the reality of Matthew 6:33. My struggle has forced me

to seek the Lord first and depend on Him
and His Word. At last, I'm able to praise
the Lord and mean it. He is with me.

19

*When Your Soul
Cries for Rest*

I said, "Oh, that I had the wings of a dove! I would fly away and be at rest" (Psalm 55:6).

*M*ost of us have felt like the psalmist who wished he could fly away and find rest. Author/lecturer Robert Johnson tells of an experience in his early life—a time when his soul and body cried out for rest. His body ached with exhaustion from having worked hard all night. But he decided that more than he needed his bed, he needed to see something of God's beauty.

Instead of heading home, he drove several miles to the top of a mountain to watch the sun rise. For a little while in the quiet beauty of the moment, he felt no tiredness. He says he became so tranquil that he "heard the stars sing." He drove home, never to be the same again.

When you feel the lack of inner rest, it might be that to find a place where you can bask in God's gift of beauty would be the best thing to do. If your situation is such that it's impossible to get away for a few hours, you might try taking a mini-vacation right where you are. Find a quiet spot, close your eyes, and simply imagine you're in a place of rest, peace, and tranquillity. Know you're not alone.

*When I said, "My foot is slipping," your love,
O LORD, supported me. When anxiety was
great within me, your consolation brought joy
to my soul* (Psalm 94:18,19).

 nxiety is the opposite of peace, rest, and joy.
Not even our bodies can rest when we feel
anxious. The psalmist knew what it meant to be
anxious. He spent many anxious moments in his
life, but he learned to find rest and consolation in
the Lord.

Several years ago a Christian magazine carried
the story of how a woman and her medically incur-
able husband were surviving his final years. One of
the most restful activities of their day was a visit to
their backyard birdhouse where several families of
martins and sparrows made their home. Watching
the birds reminded the couple that the God whose
eye is on the martins and sparrows knew their circumstances and would see them through.

Crises in our lives increase our need for inner
rest, strength, and motivation for living. You and I
can be assured of the same support and consolation
that the psalmist found. God loves us as much as

He loved the psalmist, and His power is the same. "For he is our God and we are the people of his pasture" (Psalm 95:7).

I am still confident of this: I will see the goodness of the LORD in the land of the living (Psalm 27:13).

*A*Christian woman was in such distress of soul that she even began to doubt the existence of God. She wrote to a friend for help. After several words of encouragement, her friend reminded her that the time would come when she would find rest and affirm with the psalmist the above words.

When emotional or spiritual rest seem to elude us, we may need to remind ourselves often that we can still be confident of seeing the goodness of the Lord. He loves us too much to allow us to remain in a downcast state.

Several years ago when I felt almost hopeless, I hit on the idea of writing several Scripture-based affirmations on index cards. I placed the cards in a small box until I had about 30. I kept the box on my kitchen table. At each meal I meditated on and memorized one of the affirmations. That practice firmly planted enough positive thoughts in my mind to crowd out self-destructive images.

I've also found that listening often to Christian praise music helps to lift my spirits. Most of us can receive an emotional uplift by such a daily practice.

In repentance and rest is your salvation, in quietness and trust is your strength (Isaiah 30:15).

*W*e who have experienced times when inner rest eluded us know that our physical strength seems to ebb away along with our inner rest. Isaiah, inspired by the Holy Spirit, declared that our strength comes from quietness and trust.

One day I came home from the doctor's office, having received disquieting news. I tried to pray, but about all I could say was, "Lord, help me to feel Your loving arms around me." I remained quiet a few moments. Then these words from the Bible came to my mind: "For we have heard of your faith in Christ Jesus [the leaning of your entire human personality on Him in absolute trust and confidence in His power, wisdom and goodness]" (Colossians 1:4 AMP).

Soon I realized that I had nothing to be disturbed about. I needed only to rest in the awareness that God is trustworthy, wise, and good. He was asking me to lean my whole self on Him and trust Him completely for the outcome of my situation, whatever that might be. The Lord wanted me to realize that I belong to Him, and He assumes complete responsibility for me.

So trust in the Lord (commit yourself to Him, lean on Him, hope confidently in Him) forever; for the Lord God is an everlasting Rock [the Rock of Ages] (Isaiah 26:4 AMP).

*A*ll of us need the assurance that we can lean on the Lord and not be disappointed. There is no safe place to find real rest except in the Lord. If I hope only in myself or in my circumstances or in other people, I am doomed for disappointment. God alone is our source of hope, our place of rest, our everlasting Rock, One who will never fail us.

> There is a place of quiet rest,
>   Near to the heart of God. . . .
> A place where all is joy and peace,
>   Near to the heart of God.

We have sung the familiar words of the hymn by C.B. McAfee, but then we may ask how we can draw near to that place of peace and rest. I believe the answer is in four words of the above Scripture verse: "hope confidently in Him."

Regardless of how long rest has evaded us, it's never too late to commit our cares to the Lord and hope confidently in Him, knowing that He is our Rock.

You're Never Alone

This is the rest with which You may cause the weary to rest (Isaiah 28:12 NKJV).

Too often we are so busy "serving" the Lord that we fail to hear His admonition to rest. A certain seminary professor told his class he was not going to take a summer vacation. He was too busy to let up doing things in the Lord's service.

Later the professor reread the Gospels looking for Jesus' attitude toward rest. He was surprised to find that the Gospels mentioned ten times during Jesus' three years of active ministry that He took periods of retirement—in addition, of course, to nightly rests and the Sabbath rest.

At least once in His busy ministry with His disciples, Jesus said to them, "Come with me by yourselves to a quiet place and get some rest" (Mark 6:31). Jesus knew that neither He nor His disciples could minister well without rest. When our bodies are weary, our spirits and emotions suffer, too.

Years ago, I heard a busy minister say, "I'd rather burn out than rust out." I think he finally learned through experience that he doesn't need to do either. He can rest in the Lord. How else can we know He is with us?

The LORD will fulfill his purpose for me; your love, O LORD, endures forever (Psalm 138:8).

"Relax," the physical therapist quietly reminded me again as he manipulated my hand to restore my wrist to normal use following a fracture.

I wasn't aware I had tensed my muscles again. "Tension is an automatic defense mechanism," the therapist explained. "We use it in an effort to protect ourselves when we're afraid of being hurt." But when I tensed my wrist, I interfered with what was being done for my good.

When I fail to relax in the Lord, I delay His purpose for me. I lose sight of the fact that He is with me. Sometimes I may resist what He is doing in my life, much as I resisted what the physical therapist was doing. That's when I need to recall the words of the song "Leaning on the Everlasting Arms":

> What have I to dread, what have I to fear,
> Leaning on the everlasting arms;
> I have blessed peace with my Lord so near,
> Leaning on the everlasting arms.
> Leaning, leaning, safe and secure from all
>   alarms;

You're Never Alone

Leaning, leaning, leaning on the everlasting arms.

20

*When You're
Searching for
Guidance*

Commit your way to the LORD, trust also in Him, and He shall bring it to pass (Psalm 37:5 NKJV).

*G*od has a dream for all of us. He wants to guide us in our decisions. Yet we sometimes search for His guidance, wondering if we're on the right path. We can be sure that the talents God has given us are an indication of His plan for us. He has built into each of us certain talents and abilities to use for His glory.

A speaker at a Christian conference was being bombarded with questions regarding how to find and do the will of God. Finally in exasperation the man answered, "Just go about doing good, as Jesus did."

When we commit our wills to the Lord, we can be sure of His guidance. The Lord never leaves us alone to try to figure out on our own what His will is. If we are in tune with the Lord and desire His purpose, we can be safe in listening to our own heart. God often writes His will on our hearts and then plants in our minds the desire to do the very thing we're longing to do.

You're Never Alone

God's purpose for us is not a complicated, hard-to-find will. As His children, we can trust Him to reveal His will to us in simple ways that glorify Him.

Your word is a lamp to my feet and a light for my path (Psalm 119:105).

Without the Word of God, it is impossible for us to know the will and purposes of God. His Word is a lamp for our feet. It is a guiding light for our path. If we habitually soak ourselves in Scripture, it should be relatively easy to discern the guidance of God. We'll become so attuned to His voice that we won't have to wonder long what He is saying to us about what He wants us to do. If we are about to make a mistake, His Word will alert us, and we'll know to take another path.

Jesus said, "You will know the truth, and the truth will set you free" (John 8:32). His truth will set us free to know His will. Soaking ourselves in the Word and desiring to follow God's will and only His will can set us free from our own confused emotions and impure motives.

If at any time our desires fail to line up with Scripture, we can be sure we're off track. God and His Word are always in line with each other. Always. We can trust the Lord never to leave us alone when we're searching for guidance. It is His good pleasure to make His will known to His children.

The LORD is near to all who call on him, to all who call on him in truth. He fulfills the desires of those who fear him (Psalm 145:18,19).

When we sincerely desire to know the will of God, He will surely make it known to us. He will fulfill that desire. Several years ago, a group of friends asked me to lead a series of meetings to be held in our town. I felt overwhelmed by the thought of such a responsibility. I didn't know how to answer.

Finally, I remembered the verse—"He fulfills the desires of those who fear [reverence] Him." The thought came to me to tell the Lord that if He wanted me to speak, to increase my desire to speak. Soon I got so excited about speaking that I could hardly wait to begin studying in preparation for the series of teachings.

I never doubted the Lord's guidance in that decision. The response to the meetings was gratifying beyond my expectations. I was reminded of Jesus' words: "If anyone wants to do His will, he shall know" (John 7:17 NKJV).

We can be sure that as we walk in the light that God has given us, He will supply more light as we need it. He is the Lord who directs us in the way we should go.

In all your ways acknowledge Him, and He shall direct your paths (Proverbs 3:6 NKJV).

*W*hat surer promise can we have that God will guide us in our decisions than the above? If I live in accordance with the teaching of God's Word and acknowledge the Lord in all my ways of thinking and doing, I can expect Him to reveal His will to me.

In addition to His written Word, God has provided a personal guide for us in the presence of the Holy Spirit. Jesus said, "When he, the Spirit of truth, comes, he will guide you into all truth" (John 16:13). All truth, of course, includes direction in whatever need for guidance we may have—large or small.

The Holy Spirit never speaks in contradiction to the Word. That is one sure way we can know whether the guidance we have is of God, by asking, "Is it in line with the Word of God?"

To be guided by the Holy Spirit, we need a personal, unbroken relationship with Him. If we grieve the Holy Spirit by any impurity in our lives, we cannot expect to hear Him speak clearly. The Holy Spirit leads only in paths of righteousness.

So then, it was not you who sent me here, but God (Genesis 45:8).

*T*hese are the words Joseph spoke to his brothers regarding their having sold him into slavery. Many years later, Joseph realized that God had used circumstances to place him in Egypt. God had a plan that eventually would enable Joseph to save his family and thousands of others from starvation.

God sometimes uses circumstances in *our* lives to point us in the direction He wants us to go. He may open or close a door to indicate His will.

However, there are times when God's will is done in spite of circumstances. It can be dangerous to accept circumstances as our total means of guidance. Circumstances do not stand alone. The advice of spiritually mature Christian friends can help us decide whether our circumstances can be interpreted as guidance from God. Even then, we must depend on what the Lord says in His Word.

Paul's words sometimes help me make a final decision: "Let the peace of Christ rule in your hearts" (Colossians 3:15). Am I at peace with the decision? God is our highest authority in any decision.

Never Alone

I've seen the lightning flashing,
And heard the thunder roll,
I've felt sin's breakers dashing,
Trying to conquer my soul;
I've heard the voice of Jesus,
Telling me still to fight on,
He promised never to leave me,
Never to leave me alone.

The world's fierce winds are blowing,
Temptations are sharp and keen;
I have a peace in knowing
My Savior stands between;
He stands to shield me from danger,
When earthly friends are gone.
He promised never to leave me,
Never to leave me alone.

When in affliction's valley,
I'm treading the road of care,
My Savior helps me to carry
My cross when heavy to bear,
My feet entangled with briars,
Ready to cast me down;
My Savior whispered His promise,
Never to leave me alone.

—Anonymous